Praise for *The Fostering Resilience Workbook, Elementary Edition*

The Fostering Resilience Workbook, Elementary Edition is an essential tool for educators navigating the demanding landscape of trauma-invested teaching. With powerful reflection exercises and a practical, step-by-step approach, it fosters personal resilience while equipping teachers to build meaningful connections with even the most challenging students. This transformative guide lays the groundwork for real, lasting impact—where healing and hope begin in the classroom.

—**Heather Yarbrough**, principal, Endeavor Elementary

This workbook has profoundly shaped my approach to working with high-risk youth, providing clear, actionable strategies that prioritize emotional awareness and safety. These compassionate, teacher-first methods are foundational to our district's culture, making every educator and student feel seen, heard, and valued.

—**Tonya Wilkes**, director of student services, Pocatello School District #25

This workbook is a must-have for elementary school staff seeking trauma-invested practices. It balances proactive tools to build safety and connection with clear, responsive approaches for supporting students (and yourself) through moments of dysregulation. Simple without being simplistic, it walks educators through engaging techniques that create calm and supportive classrooms where all students can thrive. This workbook is a practical, compassionate resource for every educator's tool kit.

—**Hannah Crumrine**, youth suicide prevention coordinator, Idaho Department of Education

The Fostering Resilience Workbook, Elementary Edition is the next best thing to working directly with the authors to move your staff practice in a more trauma-informed direction. This book offers practical strategies and real-world scenarios that will help educators build trust, foster safety, and nurture resilience in every learner.

—**Chance Whitmore**, principal

This wonderful guide is what every educator needs to be successful in their mission to serve students and families and thrive in their job. Thank you for this incredible resource, Kristin, Keith, and Pete!

—**Wendy Turner**, 2017 Delaware Teacher of the Year and author of *Embracing Adult SEL*

This workbook perfectly balances quality research with practical strategies. As a curriculum director, I'm excited to use this timely resource for developing high-quality, trauma-invested support systems.

—**Michelle Helmer**, director of curriculum, instruction, and technology, Silver Creek Central School District, New York

The Fostering Resilience Workbook, Elementary Edition provides opportunities for educators to build personal resilience as well as their capacity to foster resilient learners through proactive and responsive strategies. The reflective questions, practical examples, and templates provide the knowledge and skills needed to start or continue the work of supporting all students.

—**Marcee Wilburn, PhD**, Indiana IEP TA Center

This workbook is the ultimate all-in-one guide to understanding trauma and building resilience. It provides the what, the how, and the why for educators to learn from and reflect on as they foster resilience in their "tough nuggets" and themselves. Practical, inspiring, and relatable, this will be part of every educator's survival kit—just add coffee!

—**Kara Bratton, PhD**, School of Education, Concordia University Irvine

The Fostering Resilience Workbook, Elementary Edition provides commonsense approaches to social-emotional learning and trauma-informed practice through strong reflections, invitations, and real-world examples that can create immediate change in classrooms. Kristin, Keith, and Pete's expertise and compassion make this workbook an approachable must-have for new and experienced educators on the journey to meeting students' needs in a rapidly changing world.

—**Scott Carpenter**, assistant superintendent, La Grande School District, Oregon

As a principal who has engaged in trauma-invested work during the last 10 years, I highly recommend this resource to help educators grapple with how to respond to disengaged learners and increase adult morale and energy. The workbook's two-part experience provides stories to relate to and prompts to reflect on, along with a multitude of proactive and responsive strategies to implement. The team process in Part 2 breaks down a step-by-step collective response in supporting our "toughest nuggets" to ensure they thrive as learners. These tools, activities, and strategies are designed to build and sustain a trauma-invested mindset and environment and secure a culture of safety for students and staff. This workbook is a must-have for all elementary educators!

—**Celina Brennan**, principal, Salnave Elementary, Cheney Public Schools, Washington

I absolutely love this workbook! It encourages you to truly pause and reflect, which is so important in today's busy world. The strategies are practical and easy to apply right away, and each section is structured with thoughtful continuity, creating a smooth and meaningful journey. User-friendly and filled with real-life examples, this is a powerful tool I'll return to again and again.

—**Nicole Markealli**, school counselor, Spokane Public Schools, Washington

The authors of *The Fostering Resilience Workbook, Elementary Edition* meet educators exactly where they are and warmly invite them on a transformative journey of self-reflection. This workbook offers thoughtful support while seamlessly weaving in tangible exercises that engage and empower. The recommendations are both realistic and palatable, designed to foster continued skill development that helps educators become their best selves in supporting student growth. Masterfully combining deep knowledge, practical skills, and actionable applications to tackle some of the toughest challenges educators face, this workbook is an invaluable resource for anyone committed to creating a trauma-invested, compassionate learning environment where all students are valued and supported.

—**Megan Healy**, school counselor, Paso Robles Joint Unified School District, California

This workbook is a goldmine of grounding, affirming resources and trauma-invested tools that comes at a critical time in education. With grace and empathy, the authors ground us, remind us of our "cement shoes," and take us back to the central foundation of our practice. This guide gives us the tools to change how we see our students and grants an opportunity to collaborate with our teams to identify key ways we can support our "tough nuggets." I want to put this book into the hands of *all* my colleagues.

—**Laurie Curran**, elementary school counselor, Washington

The Fostering Resilience Workbook, Elementary Edition stands out as a practical resource for all adults working with youth. It aligns with our shared responsibility as educators, family members, and community members dedicated to the well-being of young people. The authors' insightful prompts and practical strategies encourage full engagement, allowing readers to reflect deeply and open their hearts and minds. Approachability and inclusiveness are woven throughout, making even the most challenging case studies and scenarios feel more accessible and manageable for all readers. The workbook effectively bridges theory and practice with actionable strategies, empowering adults to be their best selves while cultivating safe and nurturing learning environments where children can thrive.

I urge site, district, and county leaders to leverage this workbook as a year-round field guide, using it as a resource to develop a common language and build capacity across all settings. I am eager to incorporate this resource into my teacher preparation courses. It will undoubtedly equip future educators with the skills needed to foster comprehensive growth in both adults and children, underscoring that our aim is not just academic success, but the advancement of society.

—**Devon Hodgson**, school site and county office administrator and teacher preparation educator

THE FOSTERING RESILIENCE WORKBOOK

ELEMENTARY EDITION

ALSO BY THE AUTHORS

*Fostering Resilient Learners: Strategies for
Creating a Trauma-Sensitive Classroom*
by Kristin Souers with Pete Hall

• • • • •

*Relationship, Responsibility, and Regulation:
Trauma-Invested Strategies for Fostering Resilient Learners*
by Kristin Van Marter Souers with Pete Hall

• • • • •

*Creating a Trauma-Sensitive Classroom
(Quick Reference Guide)*
by Kristin Van Marter Souers and Pete Hall

• • • • •

*Trauma-Invested Practices to Meet Students' Needs
(Quick Reference Guide)*
by Kristin Van Marter Souers and Pete Hall

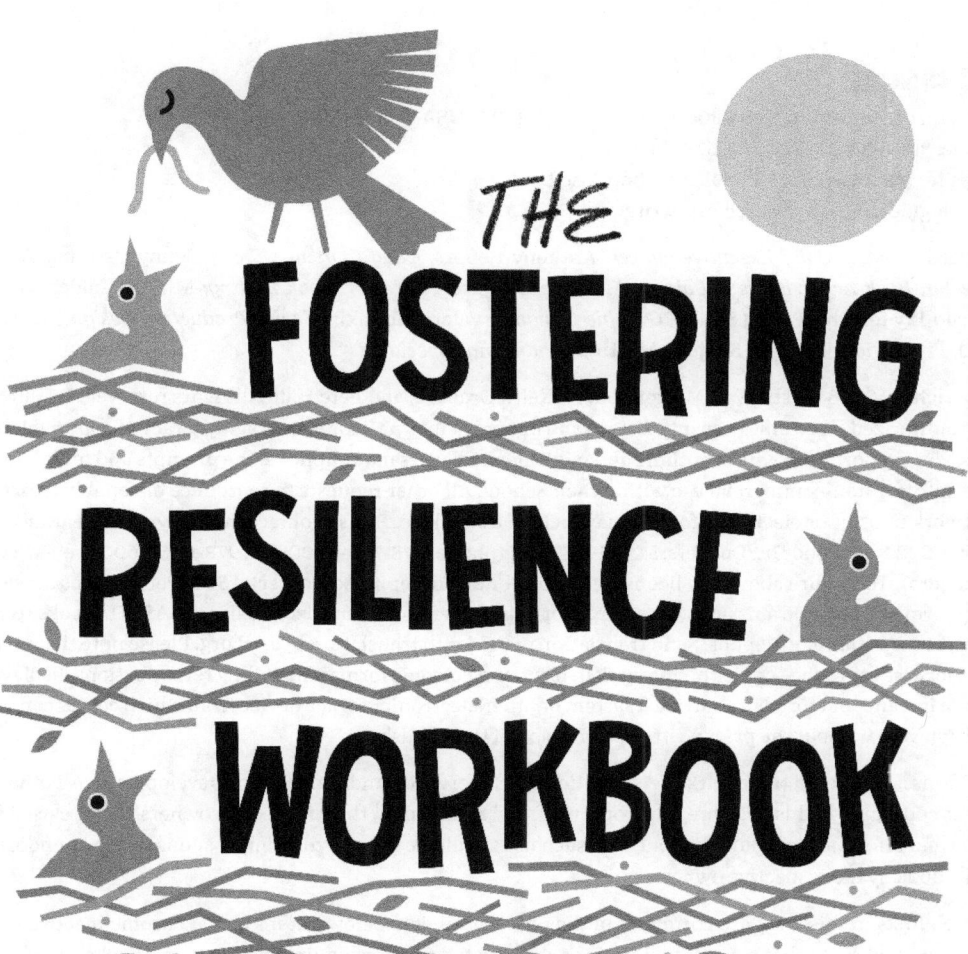

THE FOSTERING RESILIENCE WORKBOOK

STRATEGIES and STEPS to SUPPORT OUR LEARNERS

ELEMENTARY EDITION

Arlington, Virginia USA

KRISTIN VAN MARTER SOUERS KEITH ORCHARD PETE HALL

2111 Wilson Boulevard, Suite 300 • Arlington, VA 22201 USA
Phone: 800-933-2723 or 703-578-9600
Website: www.ascd.org • Email: member@ascd.org
Author guidelines: www.ascd.org/write

Richard Culatta, *Chief Executive Officer;* Anthony Rebora, *Chief Content Officer;* Genny Ostertag, *Managing Director, Book Acquisitions & Editing;* Mary Beth Nielsen, *Director, Book Editing;* Miriam Calderone, *Editor;* Donald Ely for Three Ring Studio, *Graphic Designer;* Valerie Younkin, *Senior Production Designer;* Kelly Marshall, *Production Manager;* Shajuan Martin, *E-Publishing Specialist*

Copyright © 2026 Kristin Van Marter Souers, Keith Orchard, and Pete Hall. All rights reserved. By purchasing only authorized electronic or print editions and not participating in or encouraging piracy of copyrighted materials, you support the rights of authors and publishers. Readers may duplicate the prompts and templates in the Appendix for non-commercial use within their school. All other requests to reproduce or republish excerpts of this work in print or electronic format may include a small fee. Please contact the Copyright Clearance Center (CCC), 222 Rosewood Dr., Danvers, MA 01923, USA (phone: 978-750-8400; fax: 978-646-8600; web: www.copyright.com). To inquire about site licensing options or any other reuse, contact ASCD Permissions at www.ascd.org/permissions or permissions@ascd.org. For a list of vendors authorized to license ASCD ebooks to institutions, see www.ascd.org/epubs. Send translation inquiries to translations@ascd.org. Please note that it is illegal to otherwise reproduce copies of this work in print or electronic format (including reproductions displayed on a secure intranet or stored in a retrieval system or other electronic storage device from which copies can be made or displayed) without the prior written permission of the publisher.

ASCD® is a registered trademark of Association for Supervision and Curriculum Development. All other trademarks contained in this book are the property of, and reserved by, their respective owners, and are used for editorial and informational purposes only. No such use should be construed to imply sponsorship or endorsement of the book by the respective owners.

All web links in this book are correct as of the publication date below but may have become inactive or otherwise modified since that time. If you notice a deactivated or changed link, please email books@ascd.org with the words "Link Update" in the subject line. In your message, please specify the web link, the book title, and the page number on which the link appears.

PAPERBACK ISBN: 978-1-4166-3388-4   ASCD product #125020   n10/25

PDF EBOOK ISBN: 978-1-4166-3389-1; see Books in Print for other formats.

Quantity discounts are available: email programteam@ascd.org or call 800-933-2723, ext. 5773, or 703-575-5773. For desk copies, go to www.ascd.org/deskcopy.

Library of Congress Cataloging-in-Publication Data is available for this title.
Library of Congress Control Number: 2025023641

34 33 32 31 30 29 28 27 26   1 2 3 4 5 6 7 8 9 10 11 12

To all the amazing education professionals I have had the privilege of knowing and working alongside. Thank you for ALL that you do!
—Kristin Van Marter Souers

To my loving wife, Becky, and my family for all their support, and to Pete and Kristin for taking me on as a teammate. And to Coeur d'Alene Schools for years of encouragement, guidance, and collaboration as we strive to nurture and grow all students.
—Keith Orchard

To all the committed, hopeful, and passionate educators out there, know this: It's worth it.
—Pete Hall

THE FOSTERING RESILIENCE WORKBOOK
ELEMENTARY EDITION

Introduction 1

Part 1: Building a Resilient You 9
    Introduction to Part 1 11
    Chapter 1. Wonderful, Beautiful You 13
    Chapter 2. Culture of Safety 27
    Chapter 3. Fostering Connections 40
    Chapter 4. Won't… or Can't? 55
    Chapter 5. Identifying and Meeting Fundamental Needs 65
    Chapter 6. Availability and Accountability 75
    Conclusion to Part 1 89

Part 2: Fostering Resilient Learners 91
    Introduction to Part 2 93
    Step 1. Who's the Child? 97
    Step 2. Complicating Factors and "How You Doin'?" 105
    Step 3. Culture of Safety 111
    Step 4. Fostering Connections 118
    Step 5. Won't… or Can't? 131
    Step 6. Needsleuthing 145
    Step 7. Trial and Error (and Trial and Success) 160
    Step 8. When Things Go Haywire: Response Strategies 175
    Step 9. The Bat Signal: Calling on Outside Support 197
    Conclusion to Part 2 204

Acknowledgments 206
Appendix: Prompts and Templates 207
References 254
Index 259
About the Authors 268

Introduction

Thank you.

We can think of no better way to begin this workbook than with gratitude. Thank you for the work you do every day, selflessly putting your own needs behind those of your students. Thank you for your passion and dedication to the future. Thank you for doing your best in the school trenches, working with children every day. Whether you are a teacher, a counselor, an administrator, a paraprofessional, a substitute teacher, a nurse, a specialist, a coach, a psychologist or social worker, a librarian, a tutor, a bus driver, a cafeteria worker, or a support staff member, we are thankful for your love and commitment. Let this be a reminder to you that there is *awesomeness* in all of us, and we see it in you. It is up to us as caregivers and professionals to identify and home in on that awesomeness whenever and however possible. We salute and appreciate you.

The three of us designed this workbook for you—to remind you of who you are and why you do what you do every day, and to help you do it even better. We will take you through some grounding resets and reflective questions to get you in the mindspace and the heartspace to make a difference. We'll offer tools and strategies rooted in research and experience to help you fulfill a crucial mission: bringing out the best in *all* our youth.

Welcome

Most likely, you're merging through one of two on-ramps into this workbook:

1. You might be feeling stuck with a particular student, and you need help. If you are like most, you are ready to dig in and get some advice on how to respond more effectively. You are looking for a new tool, technique, or insight that will help turn things around for this child. This is indicative of your desire to do

right by your student. You are ready for a healthy problem-solving session. If this describes you, welcome! You're in the right place.

2. Perhaps you are looking to the future, seeking long-term success by preparing your heart and mind and increasing your skills in advance. You could be a teacher, or you might be an administrator, a social worker, or a counselor who helps coach others and problem-solve sticky situations. If you're interested in learning proactive strategies to build a safe community for kids or about to start a new career, a new school year, or a new position, welcome! You are also in the right place.

If a different reason has motivated you to crack open this workbook, you, too, are welcome! We've worked in earnest to load this resource with mental models, philosophies, and reminders to stoke your self-awareness, as well as helpful tips, hints, and strategies to help you experience success and nurture the development and learning of your students.

What's in Here for You?

We organized this workbook in two parts aligning with the two on-ramps just described, but we intentionally set them in the opposite order of how we listed them. Read on and you'll understand the rationale behind this sequence.

Part 1 begins with proactive strategies: the conditions and dispositions that must be established and reinforced so that all students (and adults) can be their best selves. It is important to keep your personal motivators—*why* you do what you do—at the forefront. You can only be good to others when you're good to yourself, so this section begins with reminders of the importance of your own health—physical and emotional—as well as the need to work collaboratively to best support your students. We then transition to *how* best to do what you do, as we explore the importance of establishing a safe environment, nurturing positive relationships, understanding the neurobiology of stress, identifying and meeting fundamental needs, and creating proactive, strategic plans to support every single one of your students. It's often said that the best defense is a good offense, and having strong and consistent universal practices in place helps minimize the likelihood that students will struggle. Part 1 serves as a friendly reminder of those key foundational pieces that support students and staff as you strive to thrive (not simply survive) amid the challenges inherent to a school year.

Things don't always go as planned when working with children (or other human beings), so we then move into Part 2, our response strategies. This is where we dig in and think through the specific issues of a particular student who may need a bit more—or a bit different—support and intervention. In this section, we invite you to consider an individual student—one who is doubtlessly already on your mind, one whom you've spent many a restless night worrying about, one who tugs equally at your heartstrings and the fraying threads of your worn-out patience. We ask you questions and challenge you to think about what your "tough nugget" needs, to confront your own mindset and goals, and to unpack the motivation and skills that this young person might be lacking. We walk you through a very direct, intentional, and effective protocol as if you were sitting right next to us. You need a problem-solving partner? We're here for you. You want a deliberate plan to support a struggling student? We've got your back. You crave a concrete approach to reach a kid who's going through a tough time? We'll guide you through it. We've aimed to put all these pieces together for you as collaborators in this difficult, deeply impactful work.

Throughout Parts 1 and 2, we provide opportunities for reflective practice as well as exercises and activities to generate thinking and ways to apply what you've learned to your setting. You can engage in these reflections and exercises independently or with a team. As a bonus, many of the forms, reflections, and exercises are available in the Appendix and as downloadable PDFs that you can access as you make your way through this workbook (go to http://www.ascd.org/fostering-resilience-elementary-forms or www.fosteringresilientlearners.org/other-resources). You will be able to use and reuse these forms and exercises to address the needs of other students who cross your path.

Truly, this is a workbook. A field guide. A place for you to connect your head and your heart, to think through some complicated situations and arrive at an intentional, strategic plan that you are confident will succeed. So whenever you see a "Jot Your Thoughts" box like the one that follows, grab your pencil and record your thoughts, feelings, ideas, or whatever comes to mind in response to the prompt. Here's a friendly tip: Be honest. Write your truth. Take your time and take it seriously.

> **✏️ Jot Your Thoughts**
>
> Why am I here? What do I hope to gain from this workbook?
>
> _____
>
> _____
>
> _____

We recognize that there is no such thing as a perfect approach, nor can we create a playbook for every possible situation. Humans are complex and diverse—that's a big part of what makes us awesome! But through proactive approaches and mindsets (Part 1) and responsive strategies and plans (Part 2), this guide will help you create the conditions in which your students—each and every one of them, including your toughest nuggets—can meet their potential to succeed.

One of the cornerstones of our work is *trauma-invested practice*. To be trauma-invested is to commit "to the belief that all students have potential," be "cognizant of how stress can disrupt learning and achievement," recognize that trauma is a possibility for students and that school may be their *only* safe space, commit to providing a culture of safety, and "unite as a team and encourage one another to see the good in others and to offer grace" when necessary (Van Marter Souers with Hall, 2019, p. 27). Thus, through the lenses of kindness, fairness, belonging, and trauma-invested practice, we offer a menu of approaches, guiding questions, research, challenges, scenarios, and resources to help you and your colleagues help one another and your students manage the "mess of life" and become more resilient, better adjusted, and more successful—in school, at home, and, oh yeah: *in life*. These ideas aren't meant to replace your existing strategies, curricula, and lesson plans; they are meant to help you enhance the effectiveness of those practices. You may find validation in this process, become encouraged that you really are doing it right, and realize that sometimes it just takes patience. You may also find opportunities for growth and improvement, discovering that you need or want to revise some of your ideas to better meet the needs of those you care for. Or you may find it's time to discard a few of your "tried-and-trues" and start fresh. Odds are you will do a combination of all three!

In the end, you will walk away with a set of ideas and strategies to try, monitor, reflect on, and try again as you seek ways to help your students learn and thrive.

Your Partners in This Journey

Before you get too deep, you might like to know who is leading you through this work. We are three authors, each with distinct experiences and resources to offer. For the most part, the book is written in one voice, conveying our collective perspective and support. Occasionally in Part 1, we offer a specific story or tidbit from one author or another, as we pause to do here. Introducing Kristin, Keith, and Pete.

> **IN OUR EXPERIENCE: KRISTIN**
>
> I got into this work because I have a passion to advocate for those who have experienced struggles in their lives. In my three decades (and counting) of doing this work, I have had the privilege of working in many different fields—yet all are connected to my love of working with people. Education has been my focus for the last 10 years. I care deeply about the youth we all serve, and I believe that 100 percent of kids deserve to be seen as awesome! I have immense respect for education professionals in all roles, and I see the current struggle in education: Times are rough, behaviors are challenging, and patience and tolerance are wearing thin for many. I want to help. I have spent countless hours training, observing, and consulting with education professionals throughout the United States and across the globe. In addition to supporting these educators, I have seen some amazing teaching and gained valuable insights doing this work. I feel empowered to share these and additional ideas and suggestions in the hope that they help you in your practice. Thank you for all that you do!
>
> **IN OUR EXPERIENCE: KEITH**
>
> I have been in the "kid biz" my whole working life, starting off working at summer camps as a teenager and heading to college with the goal of becoming a high school teacher. After graduation, I landed my first professional job as a middle school teacher in Redmond,

Washington. It turns out teaching middle school is very hard, and I left pretty quickly. Although the ways I paid the bills varied, I always found myself working with kids. When I began leading backpacking trips for troubled teens in northern Idaho, I realized that what I really wanted was to be a counselor. I got my master's degree in social work and worked in many fields focused on helping those who were stuck and struggling: in family therapy with Idaho Youth Ranch, as a child welfare trainer, as a therapist for the U.S. Marines on Kaneohe Base in Hawai'i, and currently as a mental health coordinator for Coeur d'Alene Public Schools in Idaho. Throughout it all, I have studied, learned, and practiced the theories and skills for helping people learn and grow to be their best selves. For years, I have designed curriculum and professional development to help others learn about the complex realm of human motivation and behavior. These two decades of work have culminated in the ideas outlined in this workbook. I am thrilled to team up with Kristin and Pete, two bona fide superstars in the realm of trauma-invested practice for schools, to bring you a workbook that I hope will help you think, plan, problem-solve, and find the best in yourself so that you can help your students find the best in themselves.

IN OUR EXPERIENCE: PETE

Hi! I'm glad you're here. If anyone has the power, opportunity, and desire to change education, it's you. Whether you're aiming to make a difference for one kid at a time, one teacher at a time, or one school at a time, I appreciate your passion and dedication to the craft. Education is an extraordinarily challenging profession, and it's not getting easier. What I hope this workbook brings to your journey are the mindsets and practices that will help you do it better. As a former teacher and principal, I've seen the need for a resource like this, and in my work providing professional learning experiences for educators across the globe, I've seen the impact of this work done well. I'm personally grateful for my long-term partnerships with Kristin and Keith, and I'm excited to join forces with them to share this resource with you. A great tool in the hands of a committed professional makes for a work of art, and would you look at that? It's in your hands. The rest is up to you!

Together, we draw on our varied experiences—between us, we've worked in juvenile corrections, clinical therapy, the education profession (preK–12 and beyond), foster and child welfare systems, coaching, law enforcement, after-school and youth camp environments, and our own parenting—to provide you with an expert arm-in-arm companion to help you navigate these invigorating, and at times challenging, waters. We will help you set the tone for success, remind you of the power of proactive and positive practice, and guide you through the process required when things just aren't working the way you hoped they would. We acknowledge the overwhelming nature of this profession. We recognize that you are human, and you are doing the best you can with what you have in the moment. (Aren't we all!) We know that sometimes it seems tempting to give up and walk away. These times can be rough, and you're not alone. In the following pages, we remind you of the reasons why you do what you do and why you stick with it. We encourage you to have hope, to find the *awesomeness*, and to be reassured that we are a team. We are in this together.

Let's start by honoring your *awesomeness*!

Jot Your Thoughts

What skills and strengths do I bring to the role I play? When it comes to my job, what do I do really well?

_____

_____

_____

Empower Yourself

Once you dive headlong into this book, you may want to learn more about the history of adverse childhood experiences (ACEs), recent research on childhood trauma, and neurobiology and collect oodles of strategies to fill your tool kit. Please feel free to visit the website www.fosteringresilientlearners.org as well as checking out our two previous ASCD books—*Fostering Resilient Learners* (Souers with Hall, 2016) and

Relationship, Responsibility, and Regulation (Van Marter Souers with Hall, 2019)—and two Quick Reference Guides (Van Marter Souers & Hall, 2018, 2019), for access to some resources that can take you even deeper into this important work. Kristin also wrote a children's book titled *10 Things Our Brains Need* (Souers, 2024) that puts some of our concepts into language kids can understand.

Remember, human motivation is complex, and human behavior can be vexing. Although people often tend to gravitate toward a quick fix when faced with a problem, there is no one-size-fits-all approach to supporting students. This is why education can feel confusing and daunting at times.

Because each student and each situation is unique, we've developed a clear problem-solving protocol to increase the likelihood that you'll experience a breakthrough and meet your students' needs. As you think through the principles that are proven to help our young people succeed and thrive, you'll transform your own practice and increase your positive impact on all your students.

PART 1
Building a Resilient You

Introduction to Part 1

Let's take an overview of Part 1, starting at the very beginning. For students and schools to be successful, you must have robust, consistent, and universal practices (instruction and support practices applicable to all students) in place that create a *culture of safety*: a safe, consistent, and predictable environment for all, adults and young people alike. In Part 1, you'll read about the mindsets, structures, and practices that build and reinforce that culture of safety, which we refer to as a *nest*. Why a "nest"? Because this is our mission:

> Create a safe nest for students so that they learn and thrive and, when they eventually fly, they soar.

We provide examples that bring our concepts and strategies to life, and you'll interact with the text as you consider reflective questions and other prompts that challenge you to examine why and how you do what you do and what else you can do to build a better nest.

There are six elements that comprise a trauma-invested nest, no matter what your work, home, coaching, or child-rearing environment is. A brief description of each follows, and we'll unpack them together as we progress through Part 1 of this workbook.

Chapter 1: Wonderful, Beautiful You. As much as you might think this workbook is about your students, we are going to start with you! What makes you tick? What is your mission in this work? How can you maintain your own self-regulation? When it comes to creating a safe, positive nest, nothing is more important than you.

Chapter 2: Culture of Safety. In this chapter, we describe the nest in detail, exploring ways to make your setting safe, predictable, and consistent for your students.

This chapter also includes a self-assessment so you can gauge your progress and identify next steps.

Chapter 3: Fostering Connections. Most educators believe that relationships are paramount—because they are. With that understanding, we share some of our favorite proactive relationship-building strategies, imbued with empathy, the spirit of a champion, and healthy doses of repair.

Chapter 4: Won't... or Can't? Without a doubt, trauma and stress present your students with ample challenges. By understanding how the brain responds to difficult situations, you'll be better equipped to view your students' behaviors differently. The disruptive or distracting behavior in front of you might be a "can't" rather than a "won't" issue. If a student's biology and accompanying skills haven't yet developed, then it's important not to ask more of this student's brain than it has the capacity to do.

Chapter 5: Identifying and Meeting Fundamental Needs. How do you stay healthy in a stressful profession? How can you best meet your students' unmet needs that are driving their behaviors? Fear not; we share a slew of approaches for maintaining healthy, strong brains and offer a reliable protocol to help you identify what your students need most.

Chapter 6: Availability and Accountability. If you're like most educators, the question "How do I discipline kids as a trauma-invested educator?" comes up often. Here, we demonstrate how to balance the seesaw between *availability* (connecting with students on an emotional, empathic level) and *accountability* (holding students to a high standard of behavior and learning). It's not easy, *and* it's worth it.

The time has come. You're ready to investigate ways to build a more resilient you, and we're here to help. If we haven't already applauded your passion and commitment to the profession, let the echo of our cheers follow you to Chapter 1.

CHAPTER 1

Wonderful, Beautiful You

Thank you. Yes, we realize we thanked you in the Introduction, but we'd like to extend our gratitude by thanking you for bringing your *awesomeness* to work every day. You are special, and the fact that you work in this profession and share that quality with kids is worthy of celebration. It also merits some deeper investigation and discussion.

You might be thinking, *This is supposed to be a workbook about students, not me.* Well, we're here to remind you that you're the central character in this story, and to be good for kids, you've got to be good for you. One of the key things that helps us stay grounded in what we do is to remember why we do it. You got into your role for a reason, and you stay in your role for a reason.

During the last few years, we have noticed that many education professionals have lost their "why." They are getting caught up in details, mandates, and other distractors—such as loss of funding, substitute shortages, ever-evolving changes in curriculum, and pressure to "catch students up," to name a few—that make it hard for them to remember their original calling. We can't be effective in our positions when we feel stressed, overwhelmed, or unsafe. Will remembering your "why" eliminate the barrage of challenges, demands, and systemic flaws of this profession? Of course not. However, remaining mindful of your purpose is critical to building resilience so you can withstand the tough stuff—and there's always going to be tough stuff in this job.

First, Know Thyself

Great wisdom and grace start with knowing yourself. The key is to stay grounded in who you are and how you want others to experience you. We refer to this sense of groundedness as our *cement shoes,* a metaphor Kristin and Pete introduced in

Fostering Resilient Learners (Souers with Hall, 2016). What are *your* cement shoes? How will you stay grounded when the waves are attempting to pull you in and topple you over? When you're secure in your mission and sure of why you're doing what you're doing, then you're more likely to be communicating that message to others through your words and deeds. When you are struggling in your relationship or communication with another person, ask yourself whether they are experiencing your *why* in the way you intend them to. Are you staying true to your mission in your interactions with others? The following exercise is a great way to start (or continue) this self-exploration.

Jot Your Thoughts

Take a few minutes to write down the first things that come to mind when you read the following questions. We've found that limiting your responses to no more than five words for each prompt tends to make them more honest and authentic.

What is my role?

_____

_____

Who am I working for?

_____

_____

Why did I choose to become a [teacher, counselor, coach, mentor, or _____]?

_____

_____

Why do I do what I do?

_____

_____

What are my hopes for myself?
_____
_____

What do I love most about my job?
_____
_____

How do I want others to experience me?
_____
_____

What are three words I would like to be used to describe me?
_____
_____

What do I believe about children?
_____
_____

What do I value most about education?
_____
_____

What is my goal for each one of my students?
_____
_____

Reflect on your answers. Do you see any themes emerge? If you were to identify your core values, could your answers help you shape those values?

Exercise 1: Your Personal Mission

A personal mission is a statement that conveys very clearly *why* we do what we do.

Start here: Distill the most important, impactful, and influential words and phrases from the preceding Jot Your Thoughts exercise into a succinct statement that summarizes why you do what you do. In 20 words or fewer, see if you can capture the rationale and emotion behind your purpose in your profession. It may take a couple of tries, and that's OK. Be patient with yourself, because this matters.

Now seek out a trusted colleague and share your personal mission. Invite your colleague to engage in the exercise with you, too. What similarities between your missions do you notice? What differences? This is a great opportunity to discuss each of your philosophical approaches to education. As an additional challenge, ask if your colleague experiences you in a way that aligns with your mission and witnesses you embodying your mission in your interactions with others.

Finally, where can you post your mission to keep it front and center? The day-to-day grind, the exhaustion of the work, and the challenges will always be there. Will your mission statement be there to help you navigate those waters?

The Importance of Self-Regulation

Clarifying your purpose and keeping your *why* at the forefront of your mind can help you build resilience for the predictable stressors that come your way. Of course, there are *unpredictable* stressors, too, and the most unpredictable part of any environment is other people. Having your own emotions and stress in check is key to helping students—especially those who are sensitized to threat—feel calmer and safe. Thus, one of the key pieces of becoming trauma-invested and supporting your students is maintaining your own *self-regulation*. We use Blaustein and Kinniburgh's (2010) definition:

> *Self-regulation:* The capacity to effectively manage experience on many levels: cognitive, emotional, physiological, and behavioral. (p. 171)

What does this mean? Quite simply, it means we get to choose what we say, when and how we say it, the tone of voice we use, the nonverbal messages we send, and the way we present ourselves. When we are self-regulated, we can manage our responses to stimuli and ensure that when we are interacting with others, they are experiencing us in helpful, healthy, and safe ways.

When you are regulated, you can determine whether you want to contribute to the problem or to the solution. When you are dysregulated, you have no choice: you react to stimuli, often with emotions rather than rational thought. Staying regulated will ensure that your personal mission remains in your prefrontal cortex (the higher-order thinking center of your brain). By modeling your own self-regulation, explicitly teaching self-regulation strategies to students and practicing them together, and encouraging students to practice on their own and to develop self-awareness, you can build a classroom environment that is conducive to both teaching and learning.

A key to self-regulation is knowing what pushes your buttons. Have you ever found yourself in the middle of a student's outburst or another intense situation in which words, emotions, and maybe even objects were swirling around you like a tornado? In *Fostering Resilient Learners*, Kristin and Pete (Souers with Hall, 2016) referred to the importance of "staying out of Oz" in these circumstances and not "flipping your lid." (See Dr. Dan Siegel [2017] for more on lid flips and an explanation of his "hand model of the brain," which can help you and your students gain a holistic understanding of the brain that can improve your self-awareness and overall well-being.) Awareness of your buttons—the things that will most likely send you to Oz—can help you self-regulate more effectively. Being mindful of what triggers you helps you to recognize it before it pushes your buttons and, hopefully, enables you to circumvent your own "lid flip."

IN OUR EXPERIENCE: KEITH

When I was a young teacher teaching science, I hardly remembered any of the content back from when I had first learned it, so I was up late just about every night planning lessons and labs. There was no standardized science curriculum in my district, so I'd sit there with two textbooks open in front of me, vigorously attempting to put together a strong lesson for the next day. One morning, I arrived at school tired, ragged, and bleary-eyed. As I began to teach the lesson, one of my students said flatly, "This is boring."

Boom, I was triggered. I flipped my lid, and snapped in response, "Well—*you're* boring!" and that was the end of that.

In reality, the student had every right to share his feelings. My lesson might very well have been boring to him. Just because *I* thought it was great didn't mean it was objectively great. I wasn't proud of my reaction.

Sadly, this wasn't the first or only time I made such a response to students who triggered me. But after one of my not-so-flattering lid flips, I did start to engage in some reflective practice (which I continue to find helpful following any interaction that doesn't go the way I had hoped). I asked myself the following questions:

- What behavior pushed my button? "After I worked hard on a lesson, a student said, 'This is boring.'"
- What is the button? "The button is my insecurity and my fear that I'm not good enough, that I might fail. When my student said, 'This is boring,' I heard, 'You suck. You are boring. You are a bad teacher. You are failing.'"
- Why is that a button for me? "The short version of a long story is that my dad was big, strong, and tough, and I got the message for much of my early life that I just didn't measure up. My way of coping was to become 'perfect' and do everything right so that no one could accuse me of not being good enough. This meant I was, and still am, sensitive to criticism and struggle to take risks out of fear of not measuring up."
- What can I do to make that button less sensitive? "Working on myself and understanding where this button and this fear come from is a good start. Reading books and going to therapy have helped. So has working on being mindful of when this button gets pushed so I can manage my fearful reaction with some self-talk and reframes like, 'It's OK if he is bored, that is not a reflection on you,' or 'You are working hard, and even if this lesson isn't perfect, you are a good teacher and are doing enough.'"

Exercise 2: Knowing Your Buttons

Take time to reflect on some of the prompts from the preceding section.

- When was the last time I flipped my lid at work?

- What behavior pushed my button?

- What is the button? Why is that a button for me?

- How do I typically respond when that button is pushed?

- When I'm self-regulated, how do I respond instead?

- What can I do to make that button less sensitive?

- How can I recall my plan for responding when that button is pushed?

We hope this exercise has given you some insight into what affects your ability to self-regulate. It may also tap into some history for you based on your own childhood experiences. Just as you have things that trigger you, so do your students. We all find certain tones, words or phrases, behaviors, or actions harder to tolerate than others. It's also important to keep in mind that recognizing what might cause a reaction in you or your students isn't always as simple as identifying a button; it is also about recognizing internal cues that warn you that you are moving out of a regulated state.

3 Simple Ways to Enhance Your Self-Regulation Skills

In addition to engaging in reflective exercises, there are some simple strategies you can use to improve your self-regulation—starting now.

1. Mindful, deep breathing. When your brain is focused on a stressor or threat, it loses its access to thinking, planning, flexibility, and empathy. Breathing deeply in these moments does two things: First, it distracts you from the stressor, so your stress response system stops producing the chemicals that keep it activated, allowing your body to begin to calm. Second, because the body only takes deep, slow breaths when it feels safe, when you consciously and deliberately slow and deepen your breathing, you send a message to your body that you are indeed safe, and it begins the process of calming. The best way to attain the skill of mindful, deep breathing during stressful moments is to practice it when you are regulated and calm. That way, when the stressors hit, you simply need to access your muscle memory and let that breathing technique kick in. It sounds simple but takes practice, so why not practice now? Try this: Close your eyes and purposefully and mindfully slow down your next five breaths. We bet you feel a bit calmer and more relaxed. Nice work.

2. Setting intentional boundaries. One feeling we tend to crave is control, and losing that feeling can be tremendously dysregulating. Setting and adhering to realistic, intentional boundaries can help us regain that sense of control. Can you think of activities or people in your life that distract you from your purpose and drain energy and joy from you? Setting boundaries is not an easy thing to do, especially when you want to be a team player and help others, but it's important. Some of the most effective boundaries you can set include saying "no," establishing limits on the time and energy you pour into projects and events, communicating your needs to trusted allies, and asking for help when you need it. What boundaries do you need to set that can help you preserve your energy and reduce your stress both at work and outside it?

3. Focus. Have you heard the expression "You get more of what you focus on"? If so, you realize the power of your attention. Do you focus on strengths and opportunities, or do you focus on deficits and obstacles? Are you solution oriented or problem oriented? Do you sharpen your focus when you have a project to complete, giving 100 percent of your effort and attention until the work is done, or do you find yourself getting distracted and tugged away from your priorities? Assuming you get what you focus on, what are *you* focusing on? This is also a good time to ask yourself what's inside your locus of control and what isn't. Exercise 3 should help.

Exercise 3: What Can You Really Control?

Fill in the chart in Figure 1.1.

Figure 1.1 Your Locus of Control

I can't control _____, though I can control _____.

What can't I control?	What can I control?
_____	_____
_____	_____
_____	_____
_____	_____
_____	_____

What is something you notice when you compare both sides of the chart? If you recognize that the only thing you can control is yourself, the chart should reflect that. The right column might include things like what you say or do, the way you say or do it, and your facial or bodily expressions. The left column, by contrast, may include things you wish you could control and, ultimately, cannot—things like the weather, a student's behavior, the reaction of a parent or caregiver, whether someone likes you, the program budget, you name it. If you spend your time trying to control the things in the left column, you will expend precious energy that can be better used to manage the items in the right column.

Periodically in Part 1, we offer some questions designed to drive your self-reflection. You don't need to write down your answers here; we just want you to ponder the questions seriously. We've placed them in "Pause and Reflect" boxes (look for the thought-bubble icon) to prompt your thinking. If you like, take your reflections to a colleague and process them together. Here's the first one.

 **Pause and Reflect**

- How much time do I spend focusing on some of the things in the left column of Figure 1.1?
- Am I squandering precious energy thinking about, complaining about, or just generally worrying about things that are outside my control?
- Could I more effectively use this time and energy focusing on other areas?
- Which of the items listed in the right column can I spend more time cultivating?

The Power of the Reframe

When you work with young people, it's crucial to be aware of your own mindset. You began that process in Exercise 3 as you considered the limits of your control. Another factor in your mindset is a phenomenon known as your *systems of meaning* (Blaustein & Kinniburgh, 2010). Systems of meaning form when you make interpretations about events based on your own past experiences, what you have been taught to believe, and how your thoughts have been influenced by others. As a result, when you see something happen and don't know all the context, your brain fills in the blanks—say, about the motives of the individuals involved or the reason why the incident happened—in ways that may or may not be accurate. Reflexively forming and relying on your systems of meaning can lead to you inadvertently contributing to your students' behaviors.

Another factor is regulation: In *Relationship, Responsibility, and Regulation*, Kristin and Pete (Van Marter Souers with Hall, 2019) observed that when we're dysregulated, we often rely on negative systems of meaning, whereas we can access more positive systems of meaning when we're regulated and not stressed. Part of staying grounded in your "why" is being intentional about how you perceive the behavior of others and holding yourself accountable to how you may, based on your developed systems, contribute to the problem.

Fortunately, you can reframe your negative systems of meaning to more positive possibilities. Figure 1.2 lists some examples of negative thoughts and possible ways to reframe them.

Figure 1.2 Positive Reframes

Original Thought	Positive Reframe
"I've got so-and-so in my class this year. He was always in the office last year. Great."	"I know others have struggled with this student in the past. My goal is to give him a clean slate."
"The principal always gives me the behavior problems."	"My administrator/leadership teams obviously see some strength in my ability to work with tough nuggets. That said, I need to find a time to meet and ask for support."
"Everyone in that family is in special ed. I might as well start filling out the paperwork now."	"I am a good teacher, and I know I am working hard for my students."
"The only thing that will help that student is medication."	"All kids are awesome and worthy of an education."
"My evaluation depends on my test scores, and this year's bunch is low. I don't have a chance."	"The more I can learn, the better equipped I'll be to meet every child's needs."
"No one has ever gotten through to this kid. Why would I be any different?"	"Is there something I haven't tried yet that might work? Who in the building can I ask for support?"

Source: From *Relationship, Responsibility, and Regulation: Trauma-Invested Practices for Fostering Resilient Learners* (pp. 35, 37–38), by K. Van Marter Souers with P. Hall, 2019, ASCD. Copyright 2019 by Kristin Van Marter Souers and Pete Hall.

The examples in Figure 1.2 demonstrate the power of the reframe. The scenario in each row is the same, but the approaches to it are different: Whereas the statements in the left column admire the problem from an attitude of hopelessness, the statements in the right column reflect agency and open up possibilities to improving the situation.

> ## ✎ Jot Your Thoughts
>
> What do I suppose the outcomes of the "original thoughts" in Figure 1.2 might look like?
>
> _____
> _____
>
> How might the outcomes change with the "positive reframe"?
>
> _____
> _____
>
> Do I find myself defaulting to one perspective more than the other? Which one? Why?
>
> _____
> _____
>
> How might I intentionally become aware of my mindsets and systems of meaning?
>
> _____
> _____
>
> How could I shift my thinking and my perspective on purpose?
>
> _____
> _____

Who might help me in this approach?

_____

_____

IN OUR EXPERIENCE: KRISTIN

I was doing a workshop series with a team of staff, and we were talking about empathy and the importance of human connection. At the end of the day, a staff member approached me and said, "Kristin, I get the importance of relationship, but what if you just don't like a person?" She went on to share that she had a student whom she simply did not like. She wished he wasn't in her class, and she truly believed that there was no way for them to work together effectively. We talked some more and teased out her reasoning behind these strong feelings. I then asked her to try one thing: to write down at least one positive thing about this young man every day in a journal and to bring it with her when she returned for training the following month. When we met again, we talked about the assignment. She shared that she had initially felt frustrated and even angry with me, thinking there wasn't much good to say about this student. But as time passed, she found it easier to come up with positive things to write down. At the end of the conversation, she revealed that he was now her favorite student.

This is a striking example of the influence our systems of meaning and mindsets have on the connections we make with students. When we approach our struggles with a "nothing will work" perspective, then often nothing *will* work—and vice versa. In this case, as the teacher looked for positives, she started to see her student's strengths, which I fully believe had a direct effect on this student. As he began to be seen through this positive lens instead of a "troublemaking" lens, he in turn cued off his teacher's shift in focus and started to make a shift of his own, ultimately resulting in a positive connection.

Wrapping Up and Looking Ahead

We expect that as you come to the end of Chapter 1, you realize the value and importance of spending some time and energy with your mirror. The process of clarifying your mission, strengthening your self-regulation skills, knowing your buttons, and reframing your thoughts can go a long way toward setting yourself up for success. Remember, one of the most impactful elements of our students' experience we can influence is the nest—the culture of safety—and every good nest has a calm, regulated, committed caregiver. That's you! Once you've gotten into the proper headspace and heartspace to do this work, you can start looking at the nest itself. That's our focus in Chapter 2.

CHAPTER 2

Culture of Safety

Our goal is to create a nest: a safe place for kids to learn, grow, and thrive. A safe place means a consistent, predictable space that is free from fear and danger, and the foundation of any safe place is the calm presence of a predictable caregiver—you. Thus, establishing a culture of safety is essential. Without this, nothing—even the best research-based, classroom-tested strategies—will work. In *Fostering Resilient Learners*, Kristin and Pete (Souers with Hall, 2016) emphasized the importance of safety, and in *Relationship, Responsibility, and Regulation* (Van Marter Souers with Hall, 2019), we dedicated a whole chapter to the importance of establishing a culture of safety. Building a culture of safety requires adults to play nice together as a team and commit to providing this atmosphere for each and every one of their students.

In this chapter, we focus on how you can build a culture of safety by making your environment safe, predictable, and consistent.

Safe

When building a culture of safety in districts, schools, and individual settings, safety supersedes everything. For teaching and learning to thrive, students (and staff) must first feel physically and emotionally safe. As humans, our sense of safety directly affects our ability to regulate our bodies and make sound, rational decisions. When something feels unfamiliar, dangerous, or unsafe, our amygdala—the part of our brain that processes emotions, including fear and anxiety—sounds the alarm and we enter "survival mode." In this dysregulated state, we're at greater risk for making unhealthy or unsafe choices—and learning *cannot* happen.

In a culture of safety, it's important to reinforce the two crucial facets of a safe environment: physical safety and emotional safety.

Physically safe environments strive to be free of bullying, violence, threats, and harassment. Many threats to physical safety are out of your control, such as community violence, extreme weather and natural disasters, and health issues. However, through drills; plans; emergency protocols; security measures; perimeter fences; adult presence throughout the campus; and an emphasis on caring, fairness, belonging, and social-emotional awareness, you can minimize threats to physical safety in your environment.

Another aspect of a physically safe environment is the awareness that everyone in the building is committed to providing a safe space for all. Adults trust one another and can safely lean on their colleagues to share the responsibility for ensuring that safety measures are in place. In such an environment, the adults have consented to the policies and procedures for maintaining safety, and their commitment extends to every nook and cranny of the school environment.

Emotionally safe environments enable individuals to feel and express a range of emotions. In such a setting, everyone feels respected and supported, mistakes are turned into learning opportunities, and individuals feel valued for what they can contribute to the team. There is an overall feeling of inclusion, cooperation, and kindness. Emotionally safe environments welcome everyone, no matter who they are, and celebrate what makes each person unique.

Emotional safety also ensures that adults and students feel safe enough to be vulnerable with one another. All members of the school community invite others to ask for help in a judgment-free atmosphere, communicating that "we're all in this together." Adults work collaboratively to ensure that all students have opportunities to reach their potential and show their awesomeness. In turn, students know that all adults are dedicated to helping them thrive in their learning and development.

What If Something Unsafe Occurs?

Things happen, even in the safest nests we build. In a true culture of safety, harmful incidents are handled promptly to restore the environment. It is crucial that adults and students are aware of the plans and expectations for reestablishing safety, regulation, and relationship. Accountability measures for actions that violate either physical or emotional safety send a message to students, adults, caregivers, and community members about the importance of a safe and healthy environment. Rebuilding trust, repairing connections, and focusing on resolution are the primary emphases, rather than fixating on the wrongdoing. We provide ways to engage in repair in Chapter 3. (*Note:* A version of this section originally appeared in Rowe and Souers, 2020.)

> ### Jot Your Thoughts
>
> Thinking of my setting, to what extent have I focused on building a physically and emotionally safe environment for staff and all my students?
>
> _____
> _____
>
> What evidence do I have to support my answer?
>
> _____
> _____

Predictable

Predictability is the second component of a culture of safety in which all can learn, grow, teach, and thrive. The human brain, particularly the limbic system (home to our safety-seeking mechanisms and our flight-fight-freeze response), is tuned to notice what is different, irregular, and surprising. When our environment is predictable, our survival brain calms down, goes on autopilot, and allows our cerebral cortex to take charge. In schools, that's exactly where we want students to be—because that's where learning happens.

Kids who have grown up in unpredictable or unsafe environments react strongly to threats—whether those threats are real, potential, or just perceived—because that is often their mechanism for staying safe. So how can you help students who flip their lids, perceive threats in neutral situations, and struggle with change and transition? Predictability is the key.

7 Ways to Build Predictability into Your Environment

You can create a predictable and, therefore, safe environment in your school by giving yourself, your colleagues, and your students things they can count on every day, no matter what. Here's how.

1. Forecast changes. Eliminate the mystery: Be prepared to share the schedule and plan for your day upfront. Apprise students of any changes in the schedule or atypical things that may happen, like a fire or lockdown drill, an assembly, or a special visitor.

2. Establish community agreements. Setting communitywide expectations enables stakeholders in the environment to know in advance what to expect. When you have established clear norms, common expectations, and practices aimed at supporting that sense of safety in your environment, adults and students begin to develop a sense of trust. When we trust, we are more likely to regulate and stay in the thinking part of our brains.

3. Communicate clearly. Strong communication is an essential component of predictability. Everyone does better when they know what's coming next and why something is happening. Surprises move people into a dysregulated state, and even small surprises can trigger kids who come from hard places. The more communication channels and measures you have in place, the less anxious you and your students and colleagues will be. When staff, parents, students, and community members know there is a plan in place to share information, they will learn to trust that information will be provided when necessary and available. You can do this by establishing a structured plan of communication with families so they know when to expect to hear from you—for example, releasing a newsletter on the first day of each month or sending a message home every Friday. To establish clear communication with students, ensure that you provide explicit instructions that meet their developmental needs ("First, I need you to return to your desks. Then I would like you to take out a pencil. Take a deep breath and start writing on the paper in front of you about what we just learned in the story at carpet time.").

4. Plan and practice. Proactive planning for and practice of procedures also help create a sense of predictability. Reinforcing the rationale for common practices and expectations (for instance, talking with students about *why* you have protocols for evacuation drills, norms for respecting one another's personal space, and rules about freezing when the recess bell rings) helps all members commit to those practices. Likewise, explaining your intent to provide a predictable space lessens the likelihood that students will dysregulate because something wasn't stated clearly or something unexpected happened.

5. Design your space thoughtfully. Classroom setup, from the layout of furniture to the items on the walls, can also enhance the predictability of the space. Providing seating that enables students to see one another sends a message of cooperation and prepares students for opportunities to work and learn together. Offering choice (including modifications like standing stations, exercise balls, pillows, and beanbag chairs), meanwhile, allows students to feel in control and to work independently if they choose. The way you organize your space for small-group instruction, stations, transitions, and access to materials can shape students' learning experiences by creating safe traffic flow and reinforces the predictability of how bodies will be moving around the room.

6. Incorporate healthy rituals. Routines and rituals can also help your space become more predictable. What is the difference between a routine and a ritual, you ask? Routines are simply things done consistently and predictably, like the bell schedule, attendance taking, and daily announcements. Rituals are routines that incorporate the human experience by promoting connection and building relationships. For example, a morning meeting that discusses logistics and academic goals is a routine, whereas a morning meeting that invites everyone to share what they are excited about is a ritual. A greeting at the door reminding students to enter quietly and get started on their entry task is a routine. Welcoming students at the door with eye contact, a smile, and some form of connection is a ritual. The more you establish routines and rituals, the more likely it is that you will have regulated students and staff ready to engage in the learning and teaching process.

7. Foster self-regulation. Earlier, we discussed the importance of self-regulation, and it's rightfully included here as a structure and tool that increases predictability and safety. Many students come to school already dysregulated and at risk for flipping their lids. Their equanimity lasts longer on some days than on others. A student's "flipped lid moment" may have come because they could no longer hold it together, not so much because of what was happening at the time when the flip occurred; that simply may have been their tipping point. It is also important to keep in mind that some students will be more prone to "flipping their lids" than others. When you work with a student to repair your connection after the lid flip, it is important to ask, "Did something happen that made it harder for you to stay regulated and in your learning brain?" Teaching self-awareness about regulation helps with this piece. When a student can connect with their internal messaging and read the warning signs for when they are moving out of a regulated state, they can seek the support they need from you to prevent the lid flip from happening.

In your setting, you want to ensure that you are providing opportunities for students to stay regulated or to return to regulation when disrupted. You can start by establishing a common language and understanding of what regulation means. The following are ways you can promote and teach self-regulation:

- Provide signals and visuals to support students' communication with you when they are struggling with regulation. Coming up with a common language or a hand signal for students to let you know whether they are ready to learn, learning-compromised, or not learning-ready helps you know how best to support them.
- Offer regulation reset options in the classroom, like a calming corner. Having a place to go that is designed specifically for self-regulation can help a child destress. Offering simple tools like a weighted stuffed animal, headphones, a coloring book, or a fish tank might help accelerate the process and help your student return to learning more quickly.
- Engage students in activities that promote regulation support, such as brain breaks, mindfulness meditation, yoga, or core-building exercises. A strong core (the group of muscles in the midsection) promotes focus and regulation. Incorporating exercises such as rolling across a gymnastics mat, standing on one foot, or doing push-ups can support both regulation and healthy bodies.
- Teach deep-breathing exercises like belly breathing, box breathing, or "smell the flower and blow out the candle" (when the child inhales like they are smelling a flower and then blows out their breath like they are blowing out a birthday candle). Breathing helps promote regulation and focus.

Ultimately, when we think about regulation supports and overall classroom management techniques, our philosophy is "As long as it doesn't disrupt the teaching and learning of others, we are open to explore what you think will best help you learn and stay regulated."

IN OUR EXPERIENCE: PETE

As a school principal, I often found myself on the business end of a dysregulated young person. I knew my primary task was to help the student self-regulate, then to help them process the situation. One of the questions I asked my students in these situations was "What could you have done differently?" Their responses to that query confounded me because, once calm and regulated, they could rattle off a dozen or more socially acceptable, productive strategies! Incredulously, I would follow up with something along the lines of "So why the heck did you choose to throw the book, kick the teacher in the shins, and run out of the room?!"

The answer is simple. When our students are dysregulated, all those healthy choices are invisible to them. In flight-fight-freeze mode, their body's sole purpose is to avoid danger and seek safety. So I shifted my question to "What signals did your body send you that you missed?" This question is part of a concerted effort I am making to use a common language to describe what's happening in our brains and bodies. One phrase that works well is the "downstairs brain"/"upstairs brain" description we borrowed from Dr. Dan Siegel (Siegel & Bryson, 2011), clinical professor of psychiatry at the UCLA School of Medicine, and described in *Fostering Resilient Learners* (Souers with Hall, 2016). Basically, when students are stressed out, they are in the survival area of their brain, or their "downstairs brain." The higher-functioning prefrontal cortex, which enables students to think, reason, and maintain flexibility, is their "upstairs brain" and *regulates* the downstairs brain. I was able to teach students this common language as well as hand signals: thumbs-up if they're OK, fingers crossed if they need to go to the bathroom, half-raised knuckles if something is a little off in their bodies. This approach, coupled with the intentional teaching of self-regulation skills, was a game-changer in my schools.

Staying in your cement shoes—being true to your personal mission—can also provide a needed sense of predictability. When you commit to your own health and wellness, you are much more likely to be in a regulated state. When colleagues and students know you and know that you won't waver from your core self, they develop a sense of security. If you ever do become dysregulated, you take responsibility for your actions and engage in a repair—proving that you're human. When the people you interact with expect that of you, your predictability quotient increases significantly.

Providing predictability helps ensure that *everyone* will stay regulated and in the thinking part of their brains. Knowing that you cannot control all that happens is a given. Providing your students with a sense of what they can count on, no matter what, is nonnegotiable. Staying true to yourself and proactively committing to your agreed-upon practices helps to ensure that predictable space so that all can learn and thrive. (*Note:* A portion of this section originally appeared in Orchard and Souers, 2020.)

> **Jot Your Thoughts**
>
> Thinking of my setting, to what extent have I focused on building a predictable environment for staff and all my students?
>
> _____
>
> _____
>
> What evidence do I have to support my answer?
>
> _____
>
> _____

Consistent

The third component of a culture of safety is consistency. To thrive, students must be supported by daily procedures and routines that are logical, consistent, and fair. This is particularly true for students affected by trauma and toxic stress. When life outside school is chaotic, erratic, and inconsistent, it is more important than ever to create a consistent classroom environment with regular systems and supports. This means that educators clearly communicate expectations and routines and handle problems in a fair manner that makes sense. So how can you create a consistent environment?

Consistency is probably one of the hardest qualities to maintain in education. Teachers get tired, distracted, and off-kilter at times, which puts consistency at risk. For example, let's say you established a clear rule at the beginning of the year that no student is to eat crayons. Crayons are for coloring; they are not food. As the year progresses and things get stressful, you run the risk of wavering, especially if you have a particularly tough student. You may find yourself breaking your rule on a day when you are especially tired, saying, "I don't care anymore. If it's going to keep you from throwing a chair, just eat the crayon. In fact, here's a blue one!"

5 Components of Consistency in Your Environment

To help you create and maintain a consistent environment, let's look at five key components.

1. Consent across the board. One of the ingredients of a consistent environment is consent across the board. From a staff perspective, this means everyone commits to common expectations, procedures, and practices. Because there's immense value to students when adults are consistent, you will agree to certain approaches and structures *even if you don't want to*. This component isn't about teachers' comfort but about what students need to be successful. The goal is to incorporate a unified approach to helping students self-regulate first (and problem-solve second).

2. Clarity of purpose. Another way to increase consistency is to clarify the purpose and intent of your actions. When you have identified the rationale behind your goals, your students (and colleagues) will be more willing to adhere to expectations. Knowing why you're doing something is one thing—sharing that information is another. Intentionally reinforcing the *why* provides reassurance of the importance of consistent practices—and helps to align your intent with your strategies.

3. Common language. Committing to and using a common language also supports consistency, which will enhance both safety and predictability. We recommend that your building use common terms (like "downstairs brain"/"upstairs brain"), embrace a mantra that aligns with your school's mission and vision, and promote positive character traits to help reinforce to families that you are committed to the language and to the learning. For example, if you and your colleagues have taught your students about their brains and self-regulation and developed signals and tools enabling them to communicate whether they are "learning-ready," "learning-compromised," or "not learning-ready," and you are committed to using that language throughout the day, it will become a regular part of everyone's lexicon.

4. Consistent expectations. Consistent expectations also tend to breed success. Consider the use of clear learning targets. In the garden of learning in any subject, when students know what they are supposed to do and can do it, they feel successful—and their confidence and self-efficacy grow. What does partner work look like? How should students ask questions when they are unsure of something? What are students supposed to do when others are speaking? What happens in math? Do your students know the answers to these questions? Think about it: How do you feel when you know what is expected of you and you know you can make it happen? You want to do more and make that feeling last. In contrast, when expectations are unclear or inconsistent, students feel nervous and unsure of themselves and are more likely to land in their downstairs brains because of it. Avoid this by communicating clear and high expectations, revisiting them often, and reinforcing them. *Every. Single. Time.*

5. Follow-through. The fifth key component of consistency is follow-through. When you say you are going to do something, then be sure to do it. It is crucial not to overpromise. So many students have been let down by overcommitted adults. When they are taught an expectation or given a message, they want to know that there is a reason and a purpose and that they are worth it. When you follow through and commit to your promises, students are more likely to trust you and follow you on the journey. (*Note:* A version of this section originally appeared in Turner and Souers, 2020.)

Jot Your Thoughts

Thinking of my setting, to what extent have I focused on building a consistent environment for staff and all my students?

_____
_____

What evidence do I have to support my answer?

_____
_____

Exercise 4: Audit Your Nest

Now that you've read through the three components of a culture of safety, you're probably eager to assess the degree to which your students believe their environment (your common nest) is safe, predictable, and consistent. The best way to do this? Ask them.

Use the survey in Figure 2.1 to collect anonymous responses. Compile your data—using whichever data-driven dialogue protocol you're comfortable with—to identify strengths, areas of concern, and next steps.

Figure 2.1 Primary and Upper-Elementary Safety Surveys

Primary Safety Survey Questions	Never or None	Rarely or Some	Often or Most	Always or All
I feel safe in our classroom.				
I know the classroom rules and expectations.				
I can ask for help if I need it.				
My teacher tells the truth.				
I feel liked by my classmates.				
My teacher is kind to me.				
My teacher refers to our school mantra.				
I am aware of my emotions.				

Upper-Elementary Safety Survey Questions	Never or None	Rarely or Some	Often or Most	Always or All
I feel safe in our classroom.				
It is OK for me to make a mistake.				
I belong in our setting.				
All students are welcome and included in our space.				
I know how to stay safe in our classroom.				
There are structures and routines in our setting.				
We have rituals that we practice in our space.				
We have community agreements to govern our behavior.				
Members of the community adhere to the agreements.				

(*continued*)

Figure 2.1 Primary and Upper-Elementary Safety Surveys—(*continued*)

Upper-Elementary Safety Survey Questions	Never or None	Rarely or Some	Often or Most	Always or All
I practice and use self-regulation skills.				
I am aware of my emotions.				
I can communicate my emotions to others in our setting.				
We use a common language for regulation in our setting.				
I understand the purpose of everything we do in class.				
I know what I'm supposed to do (schoolwork, routines) in our setting.				
I know how I'm supposed to act (attitude, teamwork) in our setting.				
I believe that when someone in our setting says they will do something, they will do it.				

Bringing the Nest to Life: Silver Shoes

Interested in reading a bit more about a culture of safety? Read the post "Silver Shoes" on our website (www.fosteringresilientlearners.org/blog/2019/11/29/silver-shoes) for a poignant example of the motivation behind this work.

Wrapping Up and Looking Ahead

In life, we often pose the question "Is it nature or nurture?" When it comes to our students, we have literally zero control over *nature*: their DNA, their biological traits, their predispositions. However, we have a tremendous opportunity to influence *nurture*: the setting, our interactions, a culture of safety. And it's nonnegotiable. If we haven't stressed this enough, building and curating a safe, predictable, and consistent nest for our students is a foundational piece of becoming trauma-invested. In this work, without a strong culture of safety, the rest of our efforts may as well be for naught. With it, however, come the ripe conditions for establishing and fostering strong relationships—which we explore in Chapter 3.

CHAPTER 3
Fostering Connections

Do you believe that you need to have a good relationship with a student to teach them successfully? Most educators answer yes. People understand instinctively that relationships matter, and without a positive, safe, and trusting relationship, your ability to influence your student is greatly diminished.

Both students and staff learn and do their jobs more effectively when they feel important, valued, and cared for. We haven't met an educator who *doesn't* believe that relationships are essential, especially in the elementary setting. We *have* met educators who say they don't have time to build relationships, who don't always enjoy being around certain colleagues, or who struggle to connect with certain students. There are a host of factors that complicate teachers' ability to build healthy relationships with students, yet we know that without these relationships, nothing truly works. When students feel supported, they are more likely to engage in learning and are thus more likely to achieve academic success. We also know that strong relationships correlate with behaviors that are less disruptive. Bottom line: When a student is connected to at least one caring adult in the school, they do better.

Proactive Relationships—Adults First

Creating a culture of safety may have to start with the adults in the building. Hattie's (2023) research shows that one of the key indicators of success is the adults in the building playing nice together. If you haven't fostered a strong culture among your colleagues, you will certainly struggle to provide one for your students.

In the course of our work, we have seen and been told that more and more adults are pulling one another into negativity. We are seeing increasing numbers of people sporting negative mindsets about others and showing a generally unhappy, defeated attitude toward their jobs. It is heartbreaking to see, and we must start to address this as a profession. When environments start to take on this air of negativity, the overall culture and climate of the setting will suffer. That's why adults need to take the lead in fostering a collective culture of safety.

As a human being, you need emotional support just like your students do. In a collective culture of safety for adults, you have access to people who can provide a shoulder to lean on, a listening ear, encouragement, guidance, partnership, empathy, or simply companionship when (and before) you're struggling. Take a moment to reflect on how you can access these supports from your colleagues throughout the building.

Jot Your Thoughts

For each of the following prompts, write the name(s) of the person (or people) who first come(s) to mind. If you don't have a name to write, leave the space blank for now, and then ask yourself, "Who *could be* . . . ?"

_____ is my go-to support person at work.

_____ helps me regulate my emotions.

_____ helps me reframe my mindset when I am struggling with something (or someone).

_____ makes me laugh and helps support a positive culture and climate in my setting.

Being Liked vs. Being Respected

As an educator, if you had to choose between being liked and being respected, which would you pick? Write it here: It's more important to be _____. Go ahead, write it in. We'll wait.

When we poll participants at our professional development sessions, we generally get a 70/30 ratio, with "respected" coming out on top. However, this is a false choice: You can be both, and great teachers *are* both. In addition, as with all nuanced questions, the true answer is "it depends"—in this case, on the student. Some students do not need a deep connection to their teacher. They have many relationships outside the classroom, so that need is well met. Many of these students are motivated to do well and have an intrinsic desire to learn. If you earn their respect, they can be successful and learn from you.

Other students who lack connection or, more important, safety outside the classroom will need to have more than respect for you. These students need to know they are seen, heard, and valued before they can engage in the classroom community and the learning process.

Most students fall somewhere in the middle. Research (Cohen, 2022; Gopalan & Brady, 2020; Hattie, 2023) shows that when these students feel close with the adults in their school, their attendance, cooperation, and engagement improve, and they are more self-directed. This makes sense, as strong relationships lead to a sense of safety, allowing the learning brain to turn on.

You can't always control if your students like you, though you can control how you treat and approach your students. Whether a student likes or respects a teacher doesn't emerge from a vacuum, after all. Often, the teacher-student relationship relies on the adult to show respect, kindness, and a liking for the child. Do you like all your students? Educators often say they want to. If they are being honest, they know the answer might be "no" sometimes. Some kids are hard to like; they are challenging and difficult to relate to. However, if you don't work on it and find something good, decent, and likable about a student, you are in trouble (and so are they). Ultimately, our students need to know that they matter and that they are important to us.

 **Pause and Reflect**

- How important is it to me to be liked?
- Why do I think that is?
- How important is it to me to be respected?
- Why do I think that is?

> **IN OUR EXPERIENCE: KEITH**
>
> As a social worker, I would drive around northern Idaho doing family therapy for parents and their teens. These families were at risk of losing a child to juvenile corrections or child welfare, so the stakes were high! The family therapy model I used was called Functional Family Therapy, and one of its requirements was to ask the family, every two sessions, to fill out a short survey that asked questions like "How much better are you doing since you started?" and "How hopeful are you that things will change?" These are good questions measuring change and hope. The final two questions were "How much do you like and respect your therapist?" and "How much do you think your therapist likes and respects you?"
>
> Can you imagine asking your students or clients those questions on a regular basis? The rule was that if a family member responded with 7 or lower (on a 10-point scale) to either question, then therapy needed to stop temporarily: No skill building, problem solving, or homework would be effective if those feelings of respect and liking weren't solid. Instead, the therapist would say to the family, "You feel as though I don't like and respect you [or "You don't feel that you like and respect me"]. Can you tell me more about that?" The point is that without a trusting relationship, the therapy wouldn't work. The focus needed to switch from problem solving to relationship building until a safe, mutually respectful space was established.

Proactive Relationships—Students Next

Creating a nest and building a classroom community is imperative for student success. For students at all levels to stretch themselves, take risks, and dare to fail, they must feel safe with their teacher and their classmates. Fostering connections requires a little extra effort from teachers. Being nice to a student doesn't mean that you have a connection with the student. True connections take time, energy, and genuine investment in highlighting and emphasizing the messages of "I see you and *you matter*. You belong here. I am glad you are here. I care about you." These are just a few examples of messaging you can give your students. You have to be willing to model and teach these messages with each and every one of your students. Creating that culture of safety starts with emotional safety, where everyone is free to be who they are and is accepted no matter what. There are dozens of ways to build these safe and supportive classroom environments. Read on.

Exercise 5: Proactive Relationship Strategies

Figure 3.1 includes a list of actions and activities that help build strong relationships and community. Use a 1-5-10 scale to conduct an informal audit of your proactive relationship- and community-building activities. You must select either 1, 5, or 10; you cannot use the numbers in between. This forces you to commit to your choice and be prepared to defend it.

Figure 3.1 Audit of Proactive Relationship- and Community-Building Activities

1 = Never, none, or no   5 = Sometimes, some, or maybe   10 = Always, all, or yes

_____ I know my students' names and pronounce them correctly.

_____ All the students in my class know one another's names and pronounce them correctly.

_____ I am familiar with the cultures and values of all my students, and I celebrate them in my setting.

_____ I know things about my students other than their academic and behavioral status in my class (e.g., hobbies, interests, goals, likes, dislikes, family/caregiving system, pets).

_____ Students in my classroom or school have been taught explicitly what it means to be a positive member of a team and how to be a kind, helpful, and productive community member.

_____ I can identify positive things about each of my students, and I find ways to communicate about those qualities to them and their family/caregiving system (e.g., complimenting students, pointing out strengths, sending positive notes, making positive calls home).

_____ I greet each student every day by using their name, making eye contact, and offering some sort of greeting ritual (e.g., fist bump, high five, special dance, head nod, elbow bump).

_____ When a student is absent, I make sure to connect with that student on the day they return. As a class/building, we make a strong effort to ensure that students who were absent feel like they were missed.

_____ When there is a conflict in the class, I have an established plan for how to address the conflict in a safe and effective way. I have practiced this plan with my students, and they know why we do this.

1 = Never, none, or no   5 = Sometimes, some, or maybe   10 = Always, all, or yes

_____ I work hard to ensure that all my students feel accepted and valued.

_____ If a student is struggling, I have a plan in place to ensure they get the support they need.

_____ I communicate to and model regularly for all my students that I want them to feel safe coming to me for help and not to be afraid to ask questions or get their needs met.

Now review the responses that you recorded.

- If you got a 10 on any item, congratulations! This is an area of strength for you. Keep it up.

- If you got a 5 on any item, you may want to create a plan, write yourself a note, or generate some reminders to make this a more consistent practice. You can do it!

- If you got a 1 on any item, consider it a red flag. Why is that a 1? What steps can you take to move forward in this area? You may want to ask a colleague to join you in embarking on this quest together.

Top 10 Relationship-Building Strategies

In our work, we've seen a lot of great teachers, counselors, administrators, office staff, cafeteria workers, bus drivers, and others build some amazing connections with students. How do they do it? The following are the most prevalent and successful approaches we've noted, organized as a top-10 list.

1. Say my name, say my name. The first step in making students feel seen, heard, and valued is to know their names. Use their names, pronounce them accurately, and insist that students call one another by name, too. This is a foundational step in building a school culture with kindness, connection, and respect at its heart.

2. Ask for the story of their names. Have each student share their name and whatever they know about why they were given that name (first, middle, last, or nickname). Students can share information about their name's meaning, its origin, who they were named after, or anything funny or interesting about their name or nickname.

3. Adopt nicknames. Using nicknames can help students feel seen and special, particularly when the nicknames are related to an event, a characteristic, or a shared experience. Using nicknames, like calling students by name, validates students as individuals and helps to build their belonging, inclusion, and acceptance in the classroom. (*Note:* Not all kids enjoy nicknames, so use them carefully.)

4. Hold morning meetings. Anytime a class spends a little time talking about life and the world outside the curriculum, everyone has a chance to get to know each other better. *What's important to the members of the class? What's interfering with learning? What are we excited about?* Questions like these can generate terrific discussion and build connection as well.

5. Notice what's new. You can practice your observation and attunement skills every time you see your students by looking for changes. These can include outwardly noticeable changes (like new haircuts, shoes, earrings, glasses, or backpacks) and non-verbal cues (such as facial expressions, energy, emotional cues, or posture) that might open an avenue for you to show interest in individual students.

6. Play games. When students earn rewards for performing well, meeting their goals, or completing their work early, generate some excitement around celebrating with board games, puzzles, team projects, or other fun activities that incorporate collaboration, partnership, and interaction. When the reward is more social time together, your students just may flock toward one another.

7. Check in regularly. Whether you subscribe to the 2x10 strategy (spending 2 minutes a day getting to know a student for 10 consecutive days) or another approach, commit to spending a quick minute or two with as many of your students as you can as often as possible. Use this time to ask questions, monitor emotions, and demonstrate that you care.

8. Communicate with families. We've long talked about the importance of that first phone call home at the beginning of the school year. Why stop there? Make it a habit to communicate the highlights, a funny comment, a positive social interaction, a great question, or a significant demonstration of learning with your students' families throughout the year. You may be surprised by how positively everyone in the equation responds.

9. Attend events. Nothing says "I'm interested in what you're interested in" more than showing up at a game, match, recital, play, or some other student performance. Not only will you build credibility and connection, but you may enjoy the event, too!

10. Go for hugs, high fives, and handshakes. This approach became well known several years ago when a North Carolina teacher's personalized handshakes for each of his students went viral (ABC News, 2017). This strategy is effective not so much because of the intricate routines—you don't need to come up with a unique handshake for each student—but because it enables you to connect with each of your students one-on-one. Taking the time to greet each student even for a moment makes it special.

Note that physical touch isn't always possible; fortunately, connections can be forged in many ways. Eye contact and intentional wording can provide a sense of connection, and no-contact connections like waves or "air" high fives also work for students who prefer not to be touched.

Jot Your Thoughts

If I were to make this a top-11 list, what would I add? What is my most successful "go-to" connection strategy that I use with my students?

_____

_____

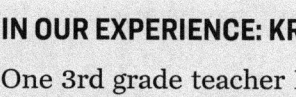

IN OUR EXPERIENCE: KRISTIN

One 3rd grade teacher I worked with created bags for her class labeled "You're Awesome." During the first week of school, each student decorated their own bag with things they wanted her to know about them: likes, interests, and favorites. She took a photo of each student and glued that onto their bag. Throughout the first part of the year, she would write positive things she noticed about each student and put the notes into the bags. When the students returned from winter break, she started having them write nice observations about each other. She would pick a student of the week, and each week all her students would write something nice about their classmate and place the notes in the student's "You're Awesome" bag. As the year progressed, the students would ask her if they could add a note to a bag based on a positive experience they had. She of course answered with a resounding *yes!*

Throughout the year, the teacher would allow students to pull out a few notes and read them. It became an incredible regulation reset for students who were struggling, and they began asking to read a note from their bags when they needed a boost.

A few years later, I ran into one of this teacher's students. I asked how she was doing and how school was going. She told me that she had had to move schools and that she had gone through some rough experiences. I asked how she was coping with all the change. She shared that she kept her "You're Awesome" bag under her pillow and that she would read those notes every night. She talked about the difference they made and the love she felt from her teacher and her class. Talk about a fabulous example of fostering connections!

Empathy First

We know that building relationships is important, and we also recognize it is not always easy to practice. Many struggling students come from places where people were or are not safe, predictable, or consistent. They have learned that people can't be trusted. Out of mere self-protection they resist connection, and rightfully so.

The key for educators is to have empathy. According to *Psychology Today*, empathy is "the ability to recognize, understand, and share the thoughts and feelings of another person" (*Psychology Today* staff, n.d., para. 1). Having empathy means that you are willing to take on the perspective of another, without shame or judgment. You are willing to "feel with" another human and send the message of "I see you, and you matter."

Sometimes our mindsets can get in the way of effective relationship building. When we view a person as difficult, resistant, scary, or troubled, we build resistance in ourselves, wishing for something different.

Ground yourself in what you know. It may just take time to earn the trust of the student. The more diligent, consistent, and safe you are, the more likely it is that the student will open up to the idea of connection.

Exercise 6: Practicing Empathy

Interpreting and practicing the term *empathy* can help you, as the adult, and your students make empathy toward one another a habit. A powerful learning tool to support this effort is *social stories*. Developed by education consultant Carol Gray (Gray & Garand, 1993), social stories, simply put, clearly demonstrate the appropriate way to behave in a given social situation. For example, say a student "flipped their lid" at recess and kicked another student. The school counselor could meet with the student and outline a social story that has the student identify healthier and safer ways to manage their anger. In essence, the student "rewrites" the story to come up with an alternative solution.

In your class, share a prompt or a social story that models empathy and ask your students to share how they would respond. Here are three examples:

> Ella just learned that her family is moving to a new city. She isn't sure how to feel about it. What is something positive or encouraging you could say to her? What is something that lets her know that change can be hard?

> Ryan was out at recess and was all by himself. What is something you could do to help him out?

> Zakariya didn't get home until late last night, and he didn't get enough sleep. He came to school grumpy. What is something you could say to Zakariya that lets him know you care?

You can also have students read social stories and then turn-and-talk with partners based on the prompts. For example, "How do you think the Man with the Yellow Hat felt when he saw that Curious George had fingerpainted his entire bedroom?" Younger students can point to a feeling on a feelings poster and share out what could cause a person to feel that way. If they saw someone with that face, what could they do to support them?

After you've tried this practice in your class, reflect on what you noticed. When you model and teach empathy to your students, do you see an impact? If so, is it positive or negative? What is something else you could try to continue teaching and practicing empathy?

Every Kid Deserves a Champion

It is important that every child in your setting has a safe connection with at least one trusted adult. *Each and every child.* One hundred percent. With great respect, we borrow a term used powerfully by the late educator Rita Pierson (2013) in her TED Talk in this pursuit: Every child deserves a *champion*. What, exactly, is a champion? Pierson's definition is a work of art: "an adult who will never give up on them, who understands the power of connection, and insists that they become the best that they can possibly be."

Some kids have multiple champions. Others may have one. Some may have none. Our responsibility as educators is to do whatever is in our power to serve as a champion for as many students as we can handle—and to ensure that every single one of our kids has at least one champion. What might that championing look like? Here are some ideas:

- A champion is kind and caring.
- A champion is in a student's corner and supports them, no matter what.
- A champion finds a way to connect with a student daily—sometimes multiple times a day, as schedules permit.
- A champion reaches out to connect with a student when the student is absent. If unable to connect, a champion finds a way to welcome the student back to school with an "I missed you" message.
- A champion prioritizes their safe relationship (asking about home, music, sports, pets, and so on) over conversations about grading and behavior. A champion is kind, nurturing, and available even when the student has misbehaved.
- A champion is a safe person with whom a student can process the messy parts of life: emotions, frustrations, struggles, getting in trouble.
- A champion emphasizes a student's awesomeness, potential, and positivity.
- A champion encourages a student to set and pursue meaningful goals with optimism and insists that they strive to be and do their very best.

Sometimes when we are consulting in a building, we ask the education professional who serves as a champion to use the power of their trusted relationship to support, guide, coach, and teach the student, and possibly to also support the adults in the building who are struggling to connect with the student in an effective way. When you are in your champion role, it is best to avoid disciplining the student whenever possible. This can be a hard line to walk at times, but the priority is to preserve the relationship. Students are most likely to keep coming back when they feel a connection to another human. Keeping the champion role clear keeps you from muddying the waters and risking a disruption in the relationship.

Most important, a champion finds a way to like and appreciate a student—to make them feel seen, heard, and valued—despite their performance. This is what can make the role so difficult and why you can't be a champion for everyone. Teachers as well as administrators and aides need their students to perform. A champion can connect with a child and enjoy them even when they are not doing well. It's not for champions to probe about behavior or academics; that is the conversation everyone else is having.

The Power and Importance of Repair

No human is perfect; despite our best intentions, we all make mistakes. That is just the reality of life. Up to this point, we've discussed how essential it is to foster connections if you want students to feel safe and thrive in your setting. That said, relationships are not always easy, and the goal is to ensure that you are safe enough and healthy enough for *100 percent* of your students. When you find yourself in a situation where a relationship is ruptured, which will inevitably happen, it is imperative to put a plan in place for repair. We have all had days when we lost our temper, missed an opportunity to connect with a person, or acted in ways that didn't align with our cement shoes. These are instances that warrant a repair.

Our definition of *repair* is as follows:

> A repair is a process in which two parties communicate very clearly that the relationship is the priority. It is a legitimate, honest, authentic reset to connection. A repair demonstrates the desire to make things better and to remain strong together.

The key to repair is simple: believing that the relationship is more important than the offense. If that's the case, proceed with a repair (which we model for you in the following paragraphs). If that's not the case—if the right-and-wrong piece feels more important than the restoration of the relationship—then a repair won't help. A repair doesn't necessarily mean there won't be a consequence or disciplinary action if a student behaved inappropriately; it simply means that in addition, you are committed to repairing the relationship and moving forward so that the choices made on both sides won't be made again in the future. If you are unwilling to commit to a true repair process, odds are you will keep encountering the same types of issues. If you find yourself stuck and unwilling to repair, it is OK to ask someone to help you get there.

Repair in Action

What does an authentic, genuine repair include? Typically, it entails the teacher modeling how to take responsibility and asking the student to do the same. It includes the words "I'm sorry," but it's not a forced apology. It's often a simple check-in with an opportunity to talk about *us,* and how whatever happened affected that connection. When there's conflict in a relationship, there must be a repair; in fact, a repaired relationship is often stronger than one that doesn't experience conflict at all. It's important to remember, though, that the repair isn't an opportunity to rehash the argument. Problem solving comes after the repair, once both parties agree that the connection is more important than the correction.

To help you picture repair in action, here's an example: Mrs. Jones was running behind in getting her 2nd grade class ready for a big test. She opted to postpone the typical morning circle and jump right into the curriculum. Tommy was not happy with this decision, and he kept raising his hand to get her attention. She asked Tommy to lower his hand and focus on the content. He continued to raise his hand. She finally yelled, "That's enough! Go sit at your desk until you can listen!" Tommy stood up, knocked over his desk, and shouted, "I was just trying to tell you that I got a cat!" He stormed out of the room. The whole class was silent.

Later that day, Mrs. Jones called Tommy into a room outside her classroom, and they sat together at a table. She said, "Tommy, I owe you an apology. I was so focused on getting us on task and learning that I forgot how important our morning meeting is to you. I am sorry that I changed the schedule without notice, and I am sorry that I got angry with you." Tommy started to cry and said, "I'm sorry I pushed over my desk and scared the class." She responded, "That is not OK behavior, Tommy, and we need to help you find a different way to show me when you are mad that is helpful, healthy, and safe." They agreed on a plan for Tommy to apologize to the class, and Mrs. Jones acknowledged that she, too, planned to apologize to the class for changing the routine. They talked for a few minutes more about Tommy's new cat and then returned to the classroom.

Relationships take time and intentional effort to build. Part of ensuring a strong connection is being able to be vulnerable and model repair when you make a mistake. Many students and even teachers have grown up in relationships where rupture occurs with no repair. That tends to result in unresolved hurt feelings and can dismantle trust. Further, it puts those affected in a position of not feeling safe and wondering when the next not-OK thing will happen.

The goal of repair is to reach a mutual understanding of what didn't go right and to establish a plan for moving forward so it doesn't happen again. Putting the importance of connection at the forefront helps students to develop a sense of trust and the ability to communicate effectively with others. Students need strong skills in connection and communication to be successful members of society. The more you model and mentor these skills, the easier it will be for students to develop the internal belief that they are both worthy of having a connection and able to provide that connection with others in a helpful, healthy, and safe way.

Jot Your Thoughts

How does the idea of repair resonate with me?

_____

_____

Does my school setting have a plan in place for repair when rupture occurs?

_____

_____

How is it working? Is it effective?

_____

_____

Are all adults in my workplace willing to engage in repair when necessary?

_____

_____

Wrapping Up and Looking Ahead

Relationships. Connection. Empathy. Champion. Repair. These are big ideas, and their success hinges on your being intentional, deliberate, and consistent with their application. Like flowers in the garden, they'll flourish with the right amount of attention and care, and they'll wilt if left unattended. Not coincidentally, when we use these approaches, our students will flourish—and when we don't, well… our students will languish.

So here we are, midway through Part 1, and we're firmly focused on how we can approach our work more purposefully and mindfully. By doing so, we're preparing ourselves to view behaviors, interactions, and incidents through a new lens in Chapter 4—one answering the question "Won't… or can't?"

CHAPTER 4
Won't... or Can't?

In this chapter, we talk about the uniqueness of humans. No two people are the same, and education professionals are adapting to many different students (not to mention colleagues) with totally different brains throughout the day. Although all teachers have routines and rituals, policies and procedures, and curriculum and instruction in place, these don't work for everybody all the time. Thus, part of your job is being patient, tolerant, and flexible in how you go about your daily interactions with others. For example, if two-thirds of your students are dysregulated at the start of the day, you are not going to jump right into the entry task; you're going to begin with a regulation reset to get kids into a learning-ready state. Better yet, you might just begin every day with a ritual that offers an opportunity for a regulation reset. In fact, we highly recommend that elementary schools incorporate these often throughout the day.

The Effects of Trauma and Stress on the Brain

Research during the last 30 years—especially the major advancements in our knowledge about the brain—has changed the way we look at students (and adults) who are struggling. If you have noticed that parenting and teaching have changed dramatically since you were a child, you are not wrong. We believe these changes are due to a much deeper understanding of the brain's physiology and chemistry. This understanding is paramount because it forms the foundation of beliefs that guide the nine-step problem-solving process we outline in Part 2. Without this knowledge, some of the questions and strategies in our model might seem odd or even counterproductive. We intentionally designed them based on our current understanding of brain science and neurobiology.

Many excellent books have been written on the impact that trauma and stress have on development, and we will not repeat those research findings here. Kristin and Pete offer a solid summary of how trauma and stress affect the brain in our first book, *Fostering Resilient Learners* (Souers with Hall, 2016). If you haven't read much about childhood trauma, we recommend that you start by looking into the Centers for Disease Control–Kaiser Permanente Adverse Childhood Experiences (ACE) study (Felitti et al., 1998). You can learn about ACEs through the Centers for Disease Control (CDC) website (www.cdc.gov/violenceprevention/aces) or the ACEs Too High website (www.acestoohigh.com). Dr. Jack Shonkoff has also done a great deal of work in this area as the founding director of the Center on the Developing Child (https://developingchild.harvard.edu). The National Child Traumatic Stress Network (https://www.nctsn.org) also offers a great deal of information on this topic.

These sites can give you a clear understanding of the impact of toxic stress on the brain and childhood development. Research continues to be released to help us understand the role that stress plays in development and the negative effect it can have on teaching and learning. We encourage you to delve into the research and extend your knowledge on these topics. It will help build your empathy and understanding and become a stronger advocate for those who are struggling.

The question we often get from education professionals at this point is *Why? Why do our students struggle so much? Why do things just seem harder for them? Why can't students just do what they are told?* You might sense intuitively that growing up in stressful environments can have a profound effect on development. However, the ACEs study demonstrated that this effect goes deeper than we may have assumed.

The brain is a complicated organ with extraordinary capacity and capability. It is also "use dependent," meaning that the parts you use will grow and develop. As you continue to use them, through patterned, repetitive experiences, they will develop stronger wiring with *myelinated sheaths*—fatty layers insulating nerve cells that enable electrical impulses to travel more quickly. This is how, through enough repetitive practice, a person can play the guitar without looking at their fingers. Their "guitar brain" has been wired and reinforced to the degree that their conscious mind no longer needs to think about the individual motions of their fingers or hands; it all takes place at a lightning-fast subconscious level. Everything we learn and can do automatically is like this, from catching a ball to reading text on a page, to name just two examples.

If a child grows up in an environment that is unpredictable, inconsistent, and potentially unsafe, or if they encounter a host of stressful experiences throughout their lives, then the stress response part of their brain—their limbic system—is being used constantly. When they are in a constant state of anticipation, waiting for the next not-OK thing, their brains stay in flight-fight-freeze mode. And because the brain is use dependent, this stress response part of their brain will develop strong wiring and become lightning-quick. Thus, students with chronic stress become sensitized to stress. Their brains are on the lookout for threat, and at the first sign of danger their stress response system kicks in, releasing a cascade of chemicals and stress hormones like adrenaline and cortisol. These can be toxic to the body when released consistently over time.

Being in this dysregulated state is not conducive to learning. A student who is in this state doesn't have access to the healthy thinking part of their brain that allows them to reason and remember effective ways to regulate. This leaves them vulnerable to behaviors that are not helpful, healthy, or safe.

The brain learns best when it feels safe. The part of the brain responsible for keeping you safe—the amygdala—is nestled in the limbic system (the stress response part of the brain). This small, almond-shaped mass is responsible for assessing the environment for threat—meaning the brains of your students are scanning you and your classroom for signs of threat or danger (Inman et al., 2023; Jha et al., 2023; LeDoux, 1996; Phelps & LeDoux, 2005; van der Kolk, 2015; Whalen et al., 2001).

IN OUR EXPERIENCE: PETE

Wendy Turner, one of our incredible colleagues and a former Delaware Teacher of the Year as well as author of *Embracing Adult SEL* (Turner, 2023), discovered a powerful way to build community while teaching her 2nd graders about the neurobiology of stress. In her classroom, she explained Dr. Dan Siegel's (2017) hand model of the brain using the "upstairs brain"/"downstairs brain" language and even taught her students the hand signals. Over time, she and her class investigated different emotions, feelings, and ways to identify and name them. There are no "bad" emotions, she would say, "just difficult ones."

> Wendy also developed a special ritual for her 2nd graders. Every morning, each student would pick one of three colored bracelets to communicate to her and the rest of the class where they were in terms of self-regulation: green for "good to go," yellow for "I'm teetering on the brink," or red for "I'm not OK right now." What a great visual to represent their social-emotional status, to communicate it to others safely and proactively, and to request support as needed. This powerful ritual really helped bond the class together (Turner, 2019).

Pause and Reflect

- When did I first become aware of the effects of trauma and stress on the brain?
- What learning have my teammates and I done in this area?
- How has this learning influenced my practice?
- What questions do I still have?

Becoming trauma-invested and taking the neurobiology of stress into account is a tall order. However, to stay true to yourself and your cement shoes, it's essential to learn as much as you can. Filling your tool belt with strategies is a great start. Shifting your mindset is a powerful next step as well. And with all this information coming in, there are three key ideas you can keep in mind when working with students.

Key Idea #1: It's Not About You

We all have moments when we say something we wish we could take back or react in anger to a student or staff member's choice. No one is perfect, and everyone makes mistakes. It is not easy to stay regulated when the person in front of you has flipped their lid, is pushing your buttons, or is acting in ways that are affecting the health and safety of your setting. Further, everyone has insecurities and fears. You might worry that you aren't good enough, that students won't appreciate you or the role you play, or that you may mess up. These fears make you human. Knowing this is key. Here is the mantra we use in such situations: *The person in front of me is doing the best they can with what they have in the moment. They are letting me know in the only way they have access to that they are "not OK." This is not about me.*

Key Idea #2: Behavior Is Communication

When students are dysregulated and struggling, they often communicate in ineffective and unhelpful ways. It is easy to get caught up in how they are showing you their dysregulation. But if you shift your focus away from "Why are you doing this?" to "What are you saying?" or "What do you need?" you can open up a world of potential. See if you can shift your mindset to the understanding that all behavior is an expression of a need. Behavior is essentially a form of communication, and it is your job to understand the need that is driving the behavior. When you create a classroom environment that is designed to support students' needs, you will minimize the likelihood of disruption and dysregulation. There are proactive things you can do to ensure that you are meeting students' needs.

Four basic needs tend to drive behavior.

1. **Physical need.** *Physical first* is the motto to remember. When a person's basic physiological or biological needs for survival are not met, they are more likely to dysregulate. You'll want to ensure that these basic needs have been met first. Are students hungry? Thirsty? Are they too hot or cold? Are they tired? Do they need to put their head down for a rest? Do they feel OK? Do they need to see the nurse?

2. **Emotional need.** These days, it feels like our entire population is crying out for their emotional needs to be met. Many of us—adults as well as kids—are struggling to get into and stay in a regulated state. Behaviors expressing emotional need can be very disruptive and overwhelming; effectively managing emotions is not an easy thing to do. Be mindful that many of your students are struggling with regulation, and ensure that you are putting some regulation reset opportunities in place throughout the day.

3. **Relational need.** People expressing relational need are typically those who rely on other people to be able to regulate. They look to others to validate and

reassure them that they are safe, they matter, and they are cared about. They have a driving need to feel a sense of belonging. Universally, we all need to feel a connection with others—some just haven't had the luxury of experiencing it in a safe or consistent way.

4. **Control need.** The chaos, unpredictability, and lack of safety associated with trauma mean that those it affects often have no control in the situation or outcome—so, naturally enough, they crave some sense of control. This can include needing to be involved in decision-making processes and taking a strong position on personal issues. Those with a strong need for control are not afraid to engage in a power struggle or assert control when they feel it's warranted. As an educator, remember that honoring someone's need for control doesn't mean you are giving up control; it means you are honoring a need.

In Step 6 of Part 2, we introduce a more detailed "needsleuthing" process designed to help students who need a bit more support. When we create an atmosphere conducive to teaching and learning, it's important to ensure that we are meeting the needs of all those we serve.

Exercise 7: Universal Approaches to Meet Students' Needs

Try implementing the universal strategies in Figure 4.1 proactively in your setting. Keep track of how your students respond to them, noticing if they help students meet their needs before (and without) feeling they need to ask for them in unhelpful, unhealthy, or unsafe ways.

After a week or so of implementation, consider the following questions:

- Which strategy did I implement? How did students respond?

- What strategies would I add to this list?

- How might I remind myself to continue these efforts to meet students' needs proactively rather than reactively?

Figure 4.1 Universal Strategies

Area of Need	Universal Strategy
Physical need	Incorporate snack, water, and movement breaks in the morning and afternoon.
Emotional need	Teach students about the brain and regulation and identify signals for them to use to communicate how they are feeling and regulating.
Relational need	Identify a "Royal Recognizer" each day who will be responsible for finding the *awesome* in each student.
Control need	Each week, have students identify a goal or a wish they have for themselves. This can be an academic/learning goal or a community service goal. At the end of the week, convene in a circle to see if students' goals were met or wishes came true.

Key Idea #3: Won't ... or Can't?

Sometimes, we confuse "I *won't* make a good choice" with "I *can't* make a good choice." Remind yourself that when you have witnessed your students making helpful, healthy, and safe choices, odds are they were in a regulated state and able to access those coping skills you worked so hard to teach them. When a student is caught off-guard or is unable to anticipate something, it can trigger an uncomfortable stress response, and into the dysregulated brain they go. Once there, they might feel compelled to do something to regain a sense of regulation, as no one truly enjoys being in this state. The student is so eager to regain some semblance of regulation and predictability that they are willing to act out in a way that could result in an exit or a consequence. The misbehavior isn't willful defiance as much as a survival response. Kids go with what they know, and comfortable doesn't always mean healthy.

Body/Mind Control in Action

Body control is a big issue in the elementary grades. Students are still working hard at developing fine and gross motor skills, communication skills, problem-solving skills, critical thinking skills, social-emotional skills, and overall academic skills. Some advance more quickly than others, and many struggle with holding still, regulating, and successfully managing their bodies in helpful, healthy, and safe ways. One key area where we universally witness struggle is lining up in the classroom. One adage we live by is "If it is predictable, it is preventable." Here are a couple of suggestions we have seen in other settings that help to minimize the incidents that tend to occur during this time:

- Put numbers in a line by the door to match the number of students in your class. Assign a student a spot to stand in for lining up at the door. Randomly place the students in these spots. When calling up table groups, assign their members to nonconsecutive numbers. This way, when they go to line up, there is less risk of pushing, running into one another, and engaging in distracting behaviors.
- When coming in from an outside activity such as recess, have students line up horizontally in their designated lines. That way, if body control is an issue, they are not slamming into the person in front of them but merely stepping into an open space. Once students are all lined up, have them take three deep breaths and then face each other's backs in a vertical line.

Remember our mantra: Students are doing the best they can with what they have in the moment. They are doing everything they can to get out of their stressed, dysregulated state. Just as we can access healthy strategies when we're regulated, regulated students are also more likely to remember expectations, behave accordingly, and ask for help in a positive way. And just like us, when they are dysregulated, students are more prone to react in ways that result in teacher frustration, loss of instructional time, and overall class disruption. This is why it is imperative to not only recognize and identify students' capacities but also provide a safe and positive learning environment.

 **Jot Your Thoughts**

When thinking about students who tend to struggle, ask these questions:

Am I asking more of this person than they have capacity to give?

_____

_____

Does this person struggle with regulation?

_____

_____

What might be causing their dysregulation?

_____

_____

Does this person have skills to be able to reset to regulation?

_____

_____

What strategies am I using to help with regulation?

_____

_____

As you reflect on these questions, it is important to be realistic in your expectations of others. You can't expect more of a brain than it has the capacity to do. If you want different, you need to teach different. If what a student is doing to manage their dysregulation is the only thing they know, then that is the only thing they'll show. Teaching a human new and more effective ways to manage their experiences takes time. It doesn't happen overnight, and you will see backward steps and mishaps as you move forward. The key is not to take the impulsive choices they make to handle their dysregulation personally. Stay grounded in who you are and how you want to be experienced, and don't get sucked into the way your student is managing their emotions in the moment.

Wrapping Up and Looking Ahead

Reframing student behaviors as (1) not a personal attack on you, (2) the expression of an unmet need, and (3) the best a child can do in the moment is a tall order, isn't it? We understand that we're really asking you to tap into your inner monologue and make some significant mindset shifts. But how you view student behaviors will determine how you respond, and if you want to respond with calmness, empathy, and a solution-oriented focus, it's important to commit to those shifts. When you're ready, we'll share some proactive strategies—for you and for your students—that will help meet your students' needs in a helpful, healthy, and safe manner. That's the focus of Chapter 5.

CHAPTER 5

Identifying and Meeting Fundamental Needs

We can't be good for others if we aren't good for ourselves. We must prioritize our own health and wellness so we can be present and regulated for the youth we serve—and, in turn, advocate for and teach our students the importance of their own wellness and self-care. When students can identify their needs and ensure they're met, they will be less likely to demonstrate their unmet needs in unhelpful, unhealthy, and unsafe ways.

10 Factors for a Strong Brain

When it comes to overall wellness, there is a strong connection between mental and physical health. When your brain and body are strong, you are more likely to remain regulated during stressful times. Educators and students alike often experience stress both at school and outside it. During the course of our work, we've uncovered research supporting 10 things that every brain needs to be healthy, happy, and prepared for success, whether in the realm of learning, work, or relationships. Here they are, in no particular order. (*Note:* A version of this list originally appeared in Hall, 2019.)

1. Sleep. On average, school-age kids need 10 hours of sleep each night, and adults need 8. During this restful time, the brain "logs off" and cleans out toxins that might lead to dementia, sorts and files important learnings and memories, and clears the path for neurons to communicate with one another (Xie et al., 2013). Encourage your students and yourself to create a bedtime ritual, snooze away, and let your brains "reboot."

2. Brain food. Not all foods are created equally; some enhance brain function better than others (Harvard Health Publishing, 2024). Many students aren't eating nutritious foods or even eating enough food to fuel their bodies at all. Further, many education professionals skip lunch to help a student or finish a lesson plan, also depriving themselves of the fuel they need to perform. Because hungry brains don't teach effectively or learn well, help yourself and your students develop healthy eating and snacking habits. Many schools provide free breakfast and lunch to ensure students don't go hungry, and some teachers go the extra mile to make sure they have snacks on hand for students who need them.

3. Water. The brain is roughly three-quarters water. Drinking sufficient water hydrates, feeds, and cleans the brain and helps it be more efficient, increasing mental alertness, processing speed, clarity, and creativity. Water also helps regulate body temperature, protects organs and tissues, and carries nutrients and oxygen to cells in the production of hormones and neurotransmitters in the brain (Shabir, 2020). Because the brain cannot store water, it's essential for you and your students to hydrate frequently.

4. Exercise. It probably comes as no surprise that regular exercise is good for you. Not only does it build strength, endurance, and overall physical health, but it has also been shown to increase volume in the prefrontal cortex and medial temporal cortex—the parts of the brain that control thinking and memory (Erickson et al., 2014). Exercise strengthens brain cells, facilitates the growth of new blood vessels in the brain, and can improve mood and sleep and reduce stress and anxiety.

5. Breathing. Engaging in deep, controlled breathing exercises (such as *pranayama* breathing, typically used in yoga, meditation, and mindfulness approaches) can help calm the brain, enhancing oxygen consumption and metabolism (Jerath et al., 2006). This decreases the likelihood of psychological or stress-related disorders, increases the brain's information processing functions, augments concentration, and improves mood.

6. Teamwork. Just like animals, brains thrive in the company of similar creatures—in this case, other brains. Humans need other humans. It seems that when people work together, cooperating to achieve a common goal, their brains tend to get "in sync" with one another (Shehata et al., 2021).

7. Challenge. When you put your brain to the test—that is, learn a new skill, vary your routines, or engage in rigorous research—you may spur *neuronal plasticity,* which prompts the growth of new brain cells, creates new connections, and generally protects against cognitive decline (Moore, 2019). Empower your students to challenge themselves, to set high expectations together, and to engage in productive struggle. When we stretch ourselves and one another, our brains work harder and get stronger, leading to increased performance across the board.

8. Limited screen time. Interested in developing your peripheral vision (which augments spatial learning, navigation, integration of information, and connections)? How about decreasing loneliness and depression? Want to sleep better? Increase mental acuity? The research in this arena is still evolving because, let's face it—screens have become ubiquitous, and our lives with them are evolving. But at this point, the preliminary consensus is that excessive screen time negatively affects all the above (Muppalla et al., 2023).

9. Laughter. When you laugh, you relieve your brain's stress response and strengthen your immune system. Laughter stimulates circulation, relieves pain, and helps us to cope when the going gets rough. Even simply smiling can help lower blood pressure, reduce stress, boost the immune system, and promote regulation (Mayo Clinic Staff, 2023; Savage et al., 2017).

10. Gratitude. Practicing gratitude improves psychological health, increases happiness and empathy, supports better sleep, and decreases aggression and the desire to seek revenge. Folks who write in a gratitude journal right before bed report sleeping better, too (Harvard Health Publishing, 2021). You can model and incorporate gratitude practices throughout the school day with your students by teaching them to hold the door for others, participating in "Fill Your Bucket" activities, and reading stories that show examples of gratitude, to name a few examples.

Exercise 8: Ways to Incorporate the 10 Factors

There are many ways you can teach and promote brain health to your students and your colleagues. We realize doing this every day is not always easy; it can be a challenge to balance all the requirements of your day-to-day expectations, and sometimes life gets messy and we get derailed from our routines. That said, having a plan in place to manage your health is essential if you want to be effective in your work, and it's possible to integrate brain health boosters into academic learning.

Pick one of the following strategies and use it consistently for a week. Pay attention to how you, your students, and your students' families respond. Does the strategy have a noticeable effect on the mood, energy, or volume of your classroom or setting? If so, why do you think it does?

- When you meet with your students, whether individually or as a class, ask them the following question as a check-in: "What is something you did this week [or yesterday or earlier today] to help your brain stay healthy?"
- Have a class challenge where students journal daily about how they incorporated the 10 factors into their day.
- Incorporate the 10 factors into your day and acknowledge them aloud as you complete them.
- When repairing with a student, use the 10 factors as an intervention tool, asking questions like "Could any of these 10 factors have contributed to the choice you made today?" "Did someone hurt your feelings?" "Are you worried about someone in your team?" "Did you eat today?" "How much sleep did you get last night?" and "Were you frustrated that I encouraged you to do a few more problems?"
- Incorporate the 10 factors into family communication, family and community events, and parent/caregiver meetings to help normalize the conversations.
- Pick a "Factor of the Week" to focus on as a class or schoolwide. For example, you might spend the week teaching and working on sleep habits.

Making the 10 Factors a Habit

On average, it takes more than two months before a new behavior becomes automatic. The length of time required for a new habit to form can also vary widely depending on the habit, the person, and the circumstances. Lally and colleagues (2010) found that it took anywhere from 18 to 254 days for people to form a new habit. There are hundreds of other studies on habits (see, for example, Duhigg, 2014), and let's just say this: Developing a new habit is not quick, and it requires focus and intentionality. Why are we talking about habits? Because it's in your and your students' best interests to habitualize behaviors based on the 10 factors so that you can meet your needs in a proactive, positive way.

Exercise 9: Self-Care Challenge

Take the Self-Care Challenge for 28 days. Record your thoughts, feelings, emotions, and baseline energy level. Keep track of the activities you engage in and how they make you feel. Figure 5.1 provides a weeklong tracker aligned to the 10 factors to get you started; a downloadable 28-day tracker is available at http://www.ascd.org/fostering-resilience-elementary-forms.

Figure 5.1 Weeklong Activity Tracker

Activity	Mon.	Tue.	Wed.	Thu.	Fri.	Sat.	Sun.
Sleep. Schedule your bedtime, turn off devices an hour before bed, and monitor your sleep.							
Brain food. Consciously decide to prepare and eat foods whose ingredients you can pronounce.							
Water. Drink 32–64 ounces of water each day, spaced out throughout the day.							
Exercise. Put in 30 minutes of heart-pumping exercise four to five times each week.							
Breathing. Learn a breathing technique and practice it every day, using it when needed.							
Teamwork. Seek out a partner to help you work, solve a problem, or brainstorm ideas.							
Challenge. Learn something new or tackle crossword puzzles, sudoku, or other brain games.							
Limited screen time. Make a concerted effort to keep your scrolling time below two hours each day.							

(continued)

Figure 5.1 Weeklong Activity Tracker—(*continued*)

Activity	Mon.	Tue.	Wed.	Thu.	Fri.	Sat.	Sun.
Laughter. Find the humor and fun in situations. Have a hearty belly laugh every day.							
Gratitude. Record two to three things you're thankful for daily in a gratitude journal, prayer, or note.							

Jot Your Thoughts

At the conclusion of the 28 days, record your responses to these questions:

How consistently did I engage in the 10 factors?

_____

_____

Which of the 10 factors was easiest for me to complete? Why?

_____

_____

Which factor did I struggle the most to complete? Why?

_____

_____

What made it easier for me to be successful?

_____

_____

How do I feel when my implementation is consistent?

_____

_____

How do I feel when my implementation is inconsistent?

_____

_____

Are these activities worth continuing? If so, can I make a personal commitment to continue them and monitor my progress?

_____

_____

7 Ideas to Strengthen the Adult Culture of Safety

We believe there are things adults can do for one another to support their collective health and wellness. The following are just a few ideas we have shared and modeled in our work with education professionals over the years.

1. Opportunities for social connectedness among staff. Providing time for staff members to connect can positively influence a school's adult culture. You can organize events during school hours (e.g., potlucks, costume days) or encourage after-school activities like forming a bowling league, signing up to walk or run a race together, or simply spending time together when the opportunity arises. We list these ideas with the recognition that everyone has a life outside work and varying demands and commitments. These activities should not be required or feel like a burden; they are simply ways staff members can connect with one another and build rapport.

2. Staff celebrations. Honoring one another's achievements is important. Celebrating weddings, new babies and grandbabies, certificates of achievement, education attainments, participation in events, athletic races, artistic performances or accomplishments, and so on is a powerful way of showing that you care about one another and your lives beyond school.

3. Positive shout-outs. Noticing one another's moments of awesomeness, big and small, can make a positive difference to the culture. You could start staff meetings with kudos or compliments for a job well done, have a shout-out bulletin board in the staff lounge for folks to post supportive notes, or place a "staff member of the week" jar in the front office where students, families, community members, and colleagues can submit words of kindness for the designated staff member.

4. Boundaries and realistic expectations. Setting and respecting realistic boundaries is so important in any career, but especially in a helping profession where caring is part of the job description. Here are some that we have found effective in creating a positive adult culture: working together to honor realistic workweeks and expectations, coming up with creative ideas to share the workload, deciding on what constitutes a realistic workday for all, turning off emails at night and on the weekends, having permission to say no when feeling overwhelmed, and developing community agreements that set expectations for how colleagues treat one another.

5. Permission to ask questions. A culture of safety honors curiosity and gives permission to seek clarity when something is confusing or seems incomplete. It is important to create a culture and climate that is free of judgment and competition. Educators' jobs are hard enough; we need to be able to rely on one another and feel safe enough to ask questions and seek support when needed. Sometimes education decisions and policies lead to confusion, frustration, and stress. Creating a culture and climate where adults are free to appropriately question and hash out such decisions increases everyone's understanding and helps colleagues figure out ways to make the changes work.

6. An "our" mentality instead of a "my" mentality. In a safe, healthy adult culture, colleagues remind one another on a regular basis that they are in this together and that each student belongs to *all* of them, not just a single teacher. Collectively, your team can do great things!

7. "Tap-in, tap-out" protocols. It's essential to put protocols in place that allow staff members to "tap out" and get a break when they need one (and staff members who have the capacity to "tap in" and help when support is needed). Healthy school cultures have systems of support that allow staff to make a phone call, go to the bathroom, reset themselves to a regulated state, or "field trip" a struggling student—an expression we coined meaning to authorize a student to visit another classroom for a set period—to give everyone in the class a break.

Jot Your Thoughts

Were any of the in-building support ideas intriguing to me? If so, which one(s), and why?

_____
_____

Can I try out one of the ideas and see how my colleagues respond?

_____
_____

Is there a support I have that wasn't mentioned above? How is it working? What do I like about it?

_____
_____

IN OUR EXPERIENCE: KRISTIN

I was working with an elementary school that was focused on enhancing its adult culture of safety. The school had gone through several staff changes, and the overall morale of the team was not high. In my training with the staff, I introduced the idea of the "tap-in, tap-out" protocol. Inspired, the 1st grade team of teachers agreed to give up their prep period one day each week and use that time to roam the halls, making themselves available to any other staff who needed assistance. Pretty soon, the other teams began to volunteer one of their prep periods each week to support their colleagues. Eventually, the teachers refined this system by posting a bulletin board in the staff lounge and developing a plan: Two staff members would be available "as needed" in response to unanticipated lid flips, and

> the others on the grade-level team on call were available to "push in" and take over a class if a teacher needed to make a phone call, repair with a student, or just use the restroom. Within six weeks, the building's culture of safety had transformed! Staff members were happier, students were acting out less, and the morale of the building as a whole was much higher.

Wrapping Up and Looking Ahead

In Chapter 1, we celebrated your awesomeness and thanked you for sharing it with your students and colleagues every day. Here, we shared key strategies for keeping that awesomeness at the forefront of your routines and mindset. This is no coincidence: The better you take care of yourself and your brain, the better equipped you'll be to care for and advocate for your students, your coworkers, and your community. Next up? Preparing yourself to handle the potentially vexing, often unpredictable, frequently disruptive behaviors your students will present to you.

CHAPTER 6
Availability and Accountability

We have observed widespread conflict and confusion in education about how to approach student discipline. Some teachers believe in just being available for their kids, holding that kindness and relationship must be at the forefront no matter what. This belief set recognizes that students may have struggles, and teachers should meet them where they are and make accommodations to support their learning whenever possible. Others believe that teachers are not "consequencing" kids enough and are too soft on them, and that students have excessive power and are getting away with too much.

Honestly, we think the movie character Forrest Gump (Zemeckis, 1994) said it best: "But I think maybe it's both. Maybe both is happening at the same time." In short, it isn't an either/or proposition. You needn't choose between being the "relationship" educator or the "discipline" educator; in fact, it's imperative that you find a way to be both. It is OK and often necessary to consequence a student, to set boundaries, and to be firm—and you can do those things while being kind. Students need to know that they matter, that they belong in their school building, and that they are destined for something awesome. They *also* need to be provided with structure, guidelines, and expectations. One of these approaches doesn't work without the other.

In the following sections, we ask you to use your trauma-invested lens to view students' behaviors a little differently than usual and to consider the unmet needs students are expressing. Children who come from hard places have sensitized stress response systems, and their responses can be challenging for adults. But it is important to maintain empathy. As we mentioned in previous chapters, these kids are doing the best they can with what they have in the moment. Remember to try and take on their perspective and understand how they are feeling and what they might need.

Now, we're the first to clarify that although the trauma-invested lens enables us to explain and understand challenging behavior, it does not excuse it. Your students need—indeed, they demand—structure and accountability alongside kindness and nurturing.

Helpful, Healthy, and Safe

One way to make this complex issue manageable is to orient your structures, expectations, and responses to three easy-to-remember categories: *helpful, healthy,* and *safe* (see Figure 6.1). When students (and adults) are engaging in behaviors that are helpful, healthy, and safe, it's likely you'll observe strong human connections and deep learning. In a setting where things are going well, you should be able to point out the choices and actions that align with the elements of the triad. Conversely, when things go awry, you can usually pinpoint which of the three elements is lacking and administer an intervention aligned with it.

Figure 6.1 Helpful-Healthy-Safe Triad

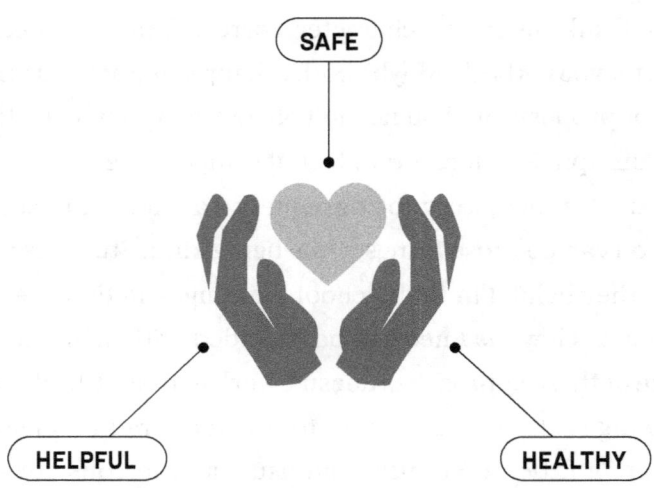

If a behavior isn't *helpful*, you can insist that a student act in a more helpful way and support them in that effort—or the consequence is a logical consequence that teaches and reinforces helpful choices. For example:

- Forgetting a pencil is not a helpful choice. An appropriate logical consequence would be for the forgetful student to sharpen the tin of spare pencils and then use one.
- A helpful choice would be showing a classmate the correct page in the book if they come in after the teacher starts reading the story.

If a student's behavior isn't healthy, you can redirect them and help them make a healthier choice—or the consequence is a logical consequence that teaches and reinforces healthy options. For example:

- Not doing your classwork is not a healthy choice because the missed learning opportunity affects your growth and development and your progression to the next skill.
- A healthy choice would be asking for a break when you start to feel dysregulated. Raising your hand and asking to get a drink of water or to take a break in the calming corner can help prevent a flipped lid.

If a student's behavior isn't safe, either you must intervene and reinstate safety, or the consequence is the student's removal from the social environment of the classroom or group. For example:

- Throwing a chair is an unsafe choice that warrants a stricter and more structured intervention, often partnered with a consequence and a plan for repair, so this behavior is no longer an option when things get hard.
- A safe choice would be to ball your fists and hold them to your side instead of throwing something, then communicating (with words or a hand signal) that you need an immediate break.

Exercise 10: Analyzing Behaviors with the Helpful-Healthy-Safe Triad

Think of some behaviors you've witnessed or experienced that disrupted the teaching and learning of others. How would you characterize them through the lens of the helpful-healthy-safe triad? Record some examples in Figure 6.2, along with some ideas for (1) logical consequences and (2) preferable options that would assist students in developing a more helpful, healthier, safer array of behaviors. Then take your notes to a trusted colleague to expand and enrich your perspective.

Figure 6.2 Analyzing Behaviors with the Helpful-Healthy-Safe Triad

Behavior	Unhelpful	Unhealthy	Unsafe	Logical Consequences and Preferable Options

We'll revisit the helpful-healthy-safe triad in just a bit. First, it's time for some serious introspection.

Balancing the Seesaw: Availability vs. Accountability

Consider the seesaw depicted in Figure 6.3.

Figure 6.3 The Balance Between Availability and Accountability

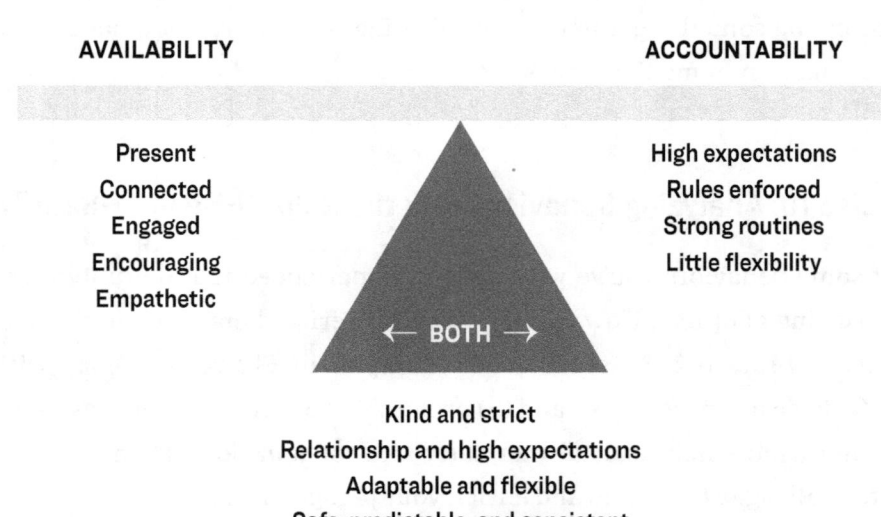

If you're too gentle and permissive, the kids will push you right off; if you're too strong and regimented, you'll smash the class into the ground. There's a sweet spot where availability and accountability are in harmony, yielding balance for you, your students, and the classroom environment. That's where the culture of safety is "just right."

So: How do *you* tend to handle misbehaviors?

Are You Too Permissive? Too Soft?

Educators who tilt this way on the seesaw often have strong relationships with their students. They like and respect their students, nurture a warm and inclusive classroom environment, and emphasize the positive. As a result, these teachers' students usually feel seen, heard, and valued. However, teachers with these strengths tend to struggle with boundaries and structure, avoid conflict, resist going the discipline route, ignore some behaviors that ought to be addressed, and attempt to redirect behavior through a mixture of asking nicely, offering choices, providing extra chances, extending grace, and, as a last resort, pleading with students. These teachers often lack either the skills or the confidence to enforce expectations consistently, so misbehaviors tend to persist and escalate, students often don't feel safe, and colleagues (and other students) may question why those kids keep getting away with breaking the rules.

Are You Too Regimented? Too Tough?

Educators on the other side of the seesaw tend to have excellent boundaries and high expectations, but they often lack empathy or warmth. Students who crave predictability often thrive in these teachers' settings because the expectations are clear and the classroom management model (misbehaviors lead to consequences) is consistent. In here, the adult is in charge. The downside that can undermine this sense of safety is the teacher's perceived unapproachability. Many students believe they must act a certain way to stay off the teacher's radar, so they are often unwilling to be vulnerable, to ask questions, to take academic risks, or to share their emotional truths. The teacher's adherence to rules and policies often runs counter to the compassion and flexibility that our toughest students need. This rigid mentality may lead students to feel blamed, shamed, scared, or embarrassed.

<!-- Jot Your Thoughts icon -->

Jot Your Thoughts

What category am I in generally with students—available or accountable?

_____

_____

If I am a parent/caregiver, what category am I in with my child? Is it the same as my category with my students? If not, what is different?

_____

_____

Do I change categories when I get stressed?

_____

_____

Thinking of an individual student in my class, do they need more structure or more nurture?

_____

_____

Getting to "Just Right"

How can you shift your approach to better balance your seesaw? There's a sweet spot where you can weave the best elements of both availability and accountability into the equation. Doing so in helpful, healthy, and safe ways will draw the best out of your students and create a "just right" culture of safety. Having an awareness of your tendencies and a desire to improve them is a fabulous way to start. Now you simply need to commit to learning and growing by identifying what your goal is, what you need to know or do differently, and how to develop and build the skill set necessary for that growth.

 **Pause and Reflect**

If you're too permissive:
- How can I use my strength and authority to draw and hold clear boundaries?
- How can I maintain order and enforce expectations while maintaining and strengthening relationships?
- How can I operate with consistency and predictability while offering flexibility and grace?

4 Strategies to Increase Accountability

If you've determined that your seesaw is tipped too far on the availability side, these four strategies will help you increase accountability.

1. Fill your tool belt. Many educators, no matter how good their preparatory program or student teaching experience was, arrive in the classroom unprepared for the reality of how young people can behave. Effectively managing a classroom and the students in it—especially in the context of high accountability for learning outcomes, curricular fidelity, and all the other professional expectations teachers face—is a tall order. The good news about developing skills is that everyone can learn them: through reading, watching videos, talking with colleagues, getting feedback from supervisors or mentors, and field-testing strategies in your classroom.

2. Know the keys to effective discipline. There are five keys to effective discipline that we discuss in further detail on pages 176–195. We developed these based on our practitioner training and experience and were inspired by the principles of Trust-Based Relational Intervention (Purvis et al., 2007; Purvis et al., 2013) as well as other discipline models. For now, here they are:

- Catch the behavior early.
- Focus on the behavior, not the person.
- Avoid power struggles.
- Respond at the right level.
- Repair and restore the relationship.

3. Build your confidence. You may have some ideas of what to say and do but lack the confidence that they will work. When it comes to self-doubt, we are often our own worst enemy. You might fear the intervention won't work, that the confrontation will wreck your relationship with the student, or that you'll be revealed as weak. Our advice is twofold: First, seek out a mentor or a trusted colleague with whom you can brainstorm strategies and practice. Second, develop and use a mantra—special words you say to yourself (and/or to your students) that convey purpose, direction, and clarity. Possible examples include "I am making a difference in the lives of my students," "I am resilient and can adapt as needed," and "My students matter." Repeating that mantra and increasing your preparation can go a long way toward building your confidence.

4. Tackle conflict head-on. You may have learned to avoid conflict and give way quite young. This tendency is possible to change, but it usually requires more time and vulnerability from you as you unpack the messages and expectations you received about conflict throughout your life. You may find that when you were younger, you weren't given a voice. Of course, having hard conversations is not easy—*and,* now more than ever, we need to be willing to have them. Some teachers worry that holding students accountable for their actions and behaviors may jeopardize or threaten their relationships and, because their classroom cultures are so heavily based on strong relationships, it will threaten the whole shebang. But it is OK to advocate for helpful, healthy, and safe. In fact, it is essential.

Pause and Reflect

If you're too regimented:

- How can I increase my flexibility to look beyond rules and policies?
- How can I practice empathy to better connect with students on an emotional level?
- How can I maintain order and control in my setting while allowing choice, offering grace, and helping students meet their needs?

3 Strategies to Increase Availability

If you've determined that your seesaw is tilted too far toward the accountability side, these three strategies will help you increase availability.

1. Realize that control is a myth. The comfort you seek in having a handle on what's going on in your setting is a compelling driver in your classroom management approach. Sometimes your craving for control and order leads to (and may stem from) a fear of losing power and authority, which can feel like the students are taking over and you are no longer managing the classroom. A better approach is realizing that just as you desire to have a say in your day, to have a voice in decision making, and to exercise options in your actions, so, too, do your students. Letting students have some control doesn't mean you're giving up control; it just means you're honoring an important student need. Allow students to make some of the decisions, to elect a path for participation, to choose a topic or a partner, or to otherwise use their voice. You're the adult, and you'll always be in charge, but the more your students own their learning, the better the environment will be.

2. Mind your mindset. You may believe that without obedience and compliance, students won't be prepared for "the real world." Rules, expectations, and consequences bring order out of chaos, and students need to follow directions to succeed. However, as it turns out, blind obedience and unilateral compliance do citizens very little good in our society. We want to prepare our students for work and careers, and it behooves them to build skills like cooperation, communication, organization, prioritization, curiosity, independence, and self-discipline, among others. Fostering this array of skills will require you to shift your thinking away from the belief set that there's only one way to do things, that debate or disagreement is insubordinate, and that multiple options lead to a free-for-all. In actuality, many possible paths can reach the same goal, debate can be healthy and eye-opening, and choice helps distribute ownership and commitment.

3. Become comfortable with emotions. If you didn't enter the profession with a warm and fuzzy personality, that's OK—it's important to honor who you are and your natural strengths and tendencies. No matter what adjectives you use to describe yourself or what words your students use to describe you, you can always lead with kindness. You can be tough and still be kind; you can discipline and still be kind; you can hold students to high expectations and still be kind; you can administer consequences and still be kind.

It's also important to practice identifying emotions with your students. Although it can feel awkward to do this, it is an essential part of learning (Osika et al., 2022); emotions play an important role in how and why students learn. When you acknowledge emotions in the classroom, you are helping to foster a supportive and safe environment conducive to learning. In your class, you can practice naming different emotions, describing them together, discussing when you and your students are feeling them, and embracing the challenge of acknowledging emotions and their role in your setting. Emotions are real, and all our students really need from us is to experience us as "safe enough, healthy enough" (Souers with Hall, 2016) to relax their guard, express themselves, and stay in a learning-ready mode.

The "Just Right" Culture in Action

Here's an example of the effort to balance availability and accountability, drawn from a school we worked in. Two seasoned teachers, one at the more regimented end of the spectrum and the other at the more permissive end, are struggling with classroom management. In the first teacher's mind, her students are out of control and disobedient. She says that 30 percent of her kids just don't care, which frustrates and angers her. She can be quick to snap at students who misbehave. We are working on shifting her mindset to find some good in all her students, specifically her toughest ones, and on softening her approach when a student needs redirection while maintaining her high standards. She is practicing bringing some lightness, humor, and warmth to her classroom, and that is helping to build safety and relationships.

The second teacher is fun and friendly, but her classroom is chaotic. Students are off task, won't listen, and talk over her. She characterizes her day as a game of "whack-a-mole," spent responding to nonstop misbehavior. Her challenge is to increase structure, starting with fundamental classroom management techniques like posting the daily schedule, developing common language, and teaching better routines. She also needs to find her voice. She often corrects a student four or five times: asking, then telling, then pleading, then yelling, and finally disciplining. Going through this process with multiple students a day is exhausting. We are working on figuring out what gets in her way of demanding (kindly) that students demonstrate kindness and respect to her. Part of it can be attributed to her personal history, and part of it is her skill set—she is just not sure what to do when a student ignores her request. Practicing strategies and having a framework to fall back on has given her a place to start and is increasing her confidence.

Exercise 11: Balancing Your Seesaw: The Two-Week Challenge

Go back to the question that started everything: How do you tend to handle misbehaviors? Which way is your seesaw tipping? Do you lean more to the permissive/soft/available side, or to the regimented/tough/accountable side? Here's the good news: To be effective in supporting your students, helping them develop self-discipline skills, and promoting a culture of safety, you need both! And you can develop both.

Now review the strategies for increasing either your accountability or your availability. Remember, you're striving for balance, designing a "just right" mentality. Try a two-week challenge:

Step 1. Write a statement that indicates what your goal is. Use these questions to guide you: *What are you trying to accomplish? What changes are you attempting to make? Why is this important to you?*

Step 2. Select a strategy and map out how you will implement it in your classroom. It may be helpful to bounce some ideas off a trusted colleague to refine your game plan before incorporating anything new or different in your setting.

Step 3. Communicate your goal and your intentions with your students. Ask them for their help, support, and partnership in this endeavor. It may surprise you how collaborative they can be if you're clear about your purpose and plan.

Step 4. Try the strategy, consistently and deliberately, for 10 consecutive school days. Record your findings, results, thoughts, and emotions in a journal or on sticky notes. If things go well, pinpoint what you did that helped usher in that success. If things go sideways, figure out which of your actions contributed to the mistakes. The more data you collect, the better you'll be able to tackle step 5.

Step 5. Compile and review your notes (perhaps with a trusted colleague to help keep you focused), identifying at least one "promising practice" (something that worked that you'll try again); one "mindset shift" (a new mental approach that you acknowledge); and one "once bitten" (a mistake you won't repeat because you've learned from it).

Step 6. Share your findings with your trusted colleague and commit to applying your learnings over the next two weeks.

IN OUR EXPERIENCE: PETE

During my years as a classroom teacher, I thought I had a pretty good recipe for managing my setting, the students, and their behaviors: Just be a nice guy! That ought to work, right? And it did—until it didn't. For the students who played the school game well, who wanted to please their teacher, who were self-driven and used healthy regulation strategies, being in a classroom with a kind, caring adult was just fine. We smiled, we engaged in activities, and we learned.

Some of my students, however, needed something different. They needed a little more structure, clearer expectations, and immediate corrections. Others needed more space, some freedom to make mistakes and learn from them, and quiet redirects afterward. If my "style" of classroom leadership didn't work for these students, they struggled. Once I learned this, I embraced two realizations: (1) Students' success is about ensuring that their needs are met, not just focusing on what I need them to do—and my students needed different things from me to be successful. (2) To accomplish the first realization, I had to identify what my students' needs were.

Did I have to become a chameleon, shape-shifting every moment to meet my students' varied needs? Heavens, no. Did I become flexible, communicating a "fair isn't always equal" mentality? Heavens, yes. Was I perfect? Heavens, no. Was that OK, because we were working through it together? Heavens, yes.

Deliberate Discipline

Before we enter this discussion, read and respond to the following Pause and Reflect prompts.

Pause and Reflect

- When I think about discipline, what does it mean to me?
- What are my goals in a disciplinary event?

Often, a conversation about discipline revolves around the behavior-consequence dyad. Educators want to know what they can do and say in the moment that will get the student to stop making life so hard. The good news is you've been reading through the proactive strategies for staying grounded, building relationships, and establishing a culture of safety, and now you're ready to respond deliberately (rather than react instinctively) to problematic behaviors.

If you're like most teachers, your response to the preceding Pause and Reflect question (*What are my goals in a disciplinary event?*) includes one or more of the following:

1. You want the behavior to change.
2. You want the relationship to remain intact.
3. You want to feel good and hopeful about future behaviors and learning.

The reality is that you will run into struggles and students will dysregulate. Within your setting, it is therefore important that your expectations are clear and your goals well known to students. The two key things you want your students to be able to do are (1) develop the skills to stay regulated and learning ready *and* (2) be helpful, healthy, and safe teammates to one another.

The safer, more predictable, and more consistent you are with your classroom expectations (this goes for building expectations as well), the more likely your students will be to follow your expectations. In Part 2, supported by a case study featuring "tough nugget" Caleb, we go into greater depth on how to work with a student who needs a bit more from you, including by walking you through using the five keys to effective discipline. As we model how these were used with Caleb, you will be able to find ways to apply them to your specific circumstances.

Exercise 12: Reflecting on Your Discipline Style

Here, we offer some heavy questions. We suggest wrestling with them in one of two ways. For option A, pick a question, any question, reflect on it, and then write your answer. Return to it the next day and ask yourself, *Is this still my answer? Now that I've slept on it, is there anything I'd change about, add to, or delete from my response?* Repeat the process for all the questions over the course of a week or two.

If you choose option B, put on your "sideline reporter" hat. Take the first question to a trusted colleague and conduct an informal interview. How does your colleague respond to the questions? What approach does your colleague take to discipline? Repeat for all the questions, interviewing multiple trusted colleagues if you can.

1. How do I handle power struggles? Going back to the idea of balancing the seesaw of availability and accountability (p. 78), am I able to achieve that balance? Do I lean one way? Do I hold students accountable and use my power when needed to keep the environment safe? Do I avoid holding students accountable when I know they are dealing with hard things outside school? Do I find myself giving multiple chances before I administer a consequence?
2. How calm am I when dealing with disrespect or defiance? Can I see the need behind that behavior and maintain a high bar for behavior while also not getting triggered myself?
3. Do I offer options and compromises within reason and in ways that are not disruptive to teaching and learning, so that a student can have some power and choice? (See Step 8 in Part 2 for more on compromise.)
4. Do I come back to students who are mad at me for holding them accountable (or for expressing frustration to them) and have a conversation and work on the repair?

After completing option A or option B, what do you notice? What themes emerge? Do your findings prompt you to think about doing anything differently in your classroom?

Wrapping Up and Looking Ahead

Ultimately, when we think of what our students need to succeed in life, we can narrow it down to two basic skills: the ability to effectively manage their emotions and the ability to connect and communicate with others. If students do not possess these two skills, they will have a difficult time finding employment, forming healthy relationships, and becoming successful contributors to their communities. Not surprisingly, we discussed these same two overarching themes throughout Part 1 as essential skills for educators. Want to be effective working with children? Learn to manage your emotions and develop your ability to connect and communicate with others.

Conclusion to Part 1

Before you turn the page and start the process of working through the challenges of a particular student, take a couple of minutes to review these Part 1 prerequisites by answering the following questions.

Chapter 1: Wonderful, Beautiful You. What did you learn about yourself as you read this opening chapter? How will that sense of self affect the way you interact with your students? How will your self-awareness influence the way your students experience you?

Chapter 2: Culture of Safety. What are you focusing on as you establish and curate your setting? To what extent are safety, predictability, and consistency emphasized in your day-to-day environment?

Chapter 3: Fostering Connections. How important are relationships to you, and what are you doing to tend to the relationships you have with each and every one of your students?

Chapter 4: Won't... or Can't? Research on stress and trauma is plentiful. How much are you taking this into consideration when working with your students? What steps are you taking to remind yourself that what's happening in front of you is likely a "can't" issue, not a "won't" issue?

Chapter 5: Identifying and Meeting Fundamental Needs. What strategies are you employing to embody the adage "Put on your own oxygen mask first" on a daily basis? How are you encouraging healthy habits for yourself and your students?

Chapter 6: Availability and Accountability. How did the metaphor of the seesaw help you notice your tendencies regarding discipline and student management? What are you going to do to try to maintain a healthy balance?

The topics and approaches we introduced in Part 1 are the prerequisites. They're what you absolutely, positively, unequivocally must have in place in every setting where you interact with students. We want our kids to experience all the awesomeness the world has to offer, and that starts with us offering awesomeness in our environments.

PART 2

Fostering Resilient Learners

Introduction to Part 2

Welcome. In our Introduction (p. 1), we explained that Part 2 of this book aligns with the first "on-ramp" into this workbook: You might be feeling stuck with a particular student, and you need help. Help is exactly what awaits you. In Part 2, we lead you through the problem-solving process we have developed for educators to use with students who confound and confuse them. In Part 1, we offered universal strategies and interventions; in Part 2, we offer ideas and interventions for students who need a little more, or a little different, support. This process will help you to get unstuck and to see a student, a situation, and even yourself a little differently. And when you see things differently, you make different decisions. You behave differently. In the end, this process will guide you toward new perspectives, new thought patterns, new actions, new plans, new interventions, and new attitudes. Who's ready for a little optimism?

A Friendly Note from Your Authors

If you skipped Part 1 because your on-ramp led you directly to Part 2, that's fine—*and* we strongly encourage you to go back and progress through Part 1. There are no shortcuts in this work, and if you haven't come to grips with wonderful, beautiful you (see Chapter 1), do so now. Ground yourself in your purpose. Reaffirm your understanding of the basics. Solidify your knowledge of the prerequisites. Then, when you're fully ready, return to Part 2.

What Can You Expect in Part 2?

We aim to serve as partners with you on this journey, so we'll walk you through our proven problem-solving process step by step (you'll notice Part 2 consists of steps instead of chapters). Referring to our fictional case study student, Caleb, throughout the nine steps, we model the process for you as thoroughly as we can in a workbook of this length. You'll be simultaneously considering one of your own students as you observe, contemplate, confront, question, brainstorm, plan, attempt, assess, and revise your thinking and your interventions to best meet your student's needs. We don't tell you what to do; rather, we provide a bit of research, a multitude of strategies, and a host of reflective questions designed to help you make informed, intentional decisions.

The process in Part 2 is one you can use iteratively and with different students. Just as each child is different, your responses to the prompts and ideas we offer will vary and lead you to design personalized plans in support of each unique, wonderful learner. As in Part 1, we've also included blank space in this workbook to allow you to reflect. Part 2's analogue to Part 1's "Jot Your Thoughts" section is "Your Turn." In this section, we invite you to introspect, record ideas, synthesize your thinking, and archive your journey.

A brief description of each step follows.

Step 1: Who's the Child? In this step, we ask you to define your goal for the student who has captured your attention. We refer to this child as a "tough nugget." This is an essential place to start, and we offer an overview of the skills, dispositions, and mindsets that tend to lead to healthy, successful members of society.

Step 2: Complicating Factors and "How You Doin'?" Here, you describe what's interfering with your student's path toward the defined goal, including behaviors, attitudes, and obstacles (the "complicating factors"). You'll examine your own thoughts, predispositions, systems of meaning, and attitudes to see how they play a role—and believe us, they do!

Step 3: Culture of Safety. You read about a culture of safety in Part 1; now it's time to examine its implementation. To what extent does your student experience a culture of safety in your classroom or school? How do you know?

Step 4: Fostering Connections. Relationships matter. To what extent does this child believe you're a committed advocate? Are you connected to this child? Is this child connected to you? Does this child have a champion?

Step 5: Won't . . . or Can't? Are you asking more of this child's brain than it can manage? Does this kid have lagging skills and unsolved problems? What skills does this child have? Which ones are they missing? Here, we share examples of how to reframe what you're seeing through the lens of trauma-invested practice, and we offer ways to remind yourself to stay cool amid the chaos.

Step 6: Needsleuthing. Here, you'll start investigating what's going on with this child. We help you "needsleuth" to determine what unmet needs your child is displaying (or which hidden needs are manifesting in various ways). We provide a clear, replicable, and effective protocol that enables you to peel back the layers of the artichoke to see what's happening at the heart of the matter.

Step 7: Trial and Error (and Trial and Success). What interventions will you implement? What will they look like? What skills do students need? What process will you use to teach them? How will you motivate students? What about motivating yourself? In this step, we provide a place to record your goals and plan, then keep track—on a weekly basis—of your intervention efforts and their results. This is where you'll log your data for six weeks.

Step 8: When Things Go Haywire: Response Strategies. Even when you are proactive, attempt to meet needs wherever you can, and otherwise do everything right, you will still have students who misbehave or struggle to meet expectations. How can you respond in the moment to help shape behavior while maintaining a safe environment? And how can you create a response system that is a bit more proactive, catching behaviors before they escalate?

Step 9: The Bat Signal: Calling on Outside Support. If you've followed the steps in the process and your student is still struggling, you might need to access extra support. Here, we give you a structure for how to bring your concerns to a team of other caring professional adults—and we walk the team through a similar process, eliciting feedback, suggestions, and perspectives from multiple people. After all, more complex problems require more complex solutions.

As you may have noticed, the nine steps in Part 2 are closely aligned with the six chapters in Part 1. In fact, there's a significant, intentional overlap. This table shows the relationship:

Part 1	Part 2
Chapter 1: Wonderful, Beautiful You	**Step 1:** Who's the Child?
	Step 2: Complicating Factors and "How You Doin'?"
Chapter 2: Culture of Safety	**Step 3:** Culture of Safety
Chapter 3: Fostering Connections	**Step 4:** Fostering Connections

Part 1	Part 2
Chapter 4: Won't… or Can't?	**Step 5:** Won't… or Can't?
Chapter 5: Identifying and Meeting Fundamental Needs	**Step 6:** Needsleuthing
Chapter 6: Availability and Accountability	**Step 7:** Trial and Error (and Trial and Success) **Step 8:** When Things Go Haywire: Response Strategies
	Step 9: The Bat Signal: Calling on Outside Support

Ready? Let's do this!

STEP 1

Who's the Child?

Here we go. Now is the time to choose a student on whom you wish to focus your supportive energy. Who is currently on your mind? Who is tricky and challenging? Who has a place in your heart but is on shakier ground when it comes to a place in your classroom or school?

A word of advice: Picking the right student is important. If this is your first time using this workbook and protocol, we recommend getting your feet wet by practicing with a student who is not your very toughest nugget. Every school has some students whose needs are extremely challenging to meet. Although we would use this same protocol with these students, it is best to learn and practice the protocol with a student with whom you are more likely to experience success. You will be more effective, feel more encouraged, and, as you gain understanding and skill, be able to apply your increased level of competence to your trickiest kiddos.

First, Identify Your Student

Who's your tough nugget? Write down the student's name or, better yet, an alias or pseudonym to ensure confidentiality: _____

OK, you've chosen your student. Our first question is this: How would you describe this young person? Before you answer, we'll offer you more specific prompts, and we're going to start with strengths. In our experience, most educators and teams are adept at describing problems and maladjusted behaviors, often in painful detail. We've been in hundreds of team meetings that devoted the first 25 minutes to defining the issue and the last 5 minutes to frantic problem solving. We want to flip the script.

Meet Caleb

This seems like the perfect time to introduce you to our "case study" student who will help you envision the application of the ideas and strategies shared here. Our fictional yet true-to-life student is named Caleb. Caleb is a 3rd grader who transferred to the school in the middle of last year. He is a bit behind in academics, but that is not the main issue. Behaviorally, he can be tough and disruptive. He has a few friends and experiences some good and productive days, but those days are not the norm. On a normal day, at best, he just refuses to work, which his teacher can ignore when she has more pressing tasks. Other times, Caleb leaves the class without permission or wanders around the classroom disrupting others. These behaviors can't be ignored and take a lot of time and energy from his classroom teacher and other adults in the school.

As you consider Caleb, we want you to imagine he's a student of yours. Even if the descriptions, behaviors, and situations don't exactly match those in your work setting and experience, we encourage you to make the necessary adaptations in your mind so that the examples better resonate.

Caleb's teacher, Ms. Coombs, is in her fifth year of teaching. Ms. Coombs is very good at building relationships, and she is also generally able to find strengths in all her students, even the tough ones. This year, though, she is feeling burned out and frustrated, and it is only November. She has a full 3rd grade classroom with many personalities, but one stands out at the top of her list of stressors. She comes to us to discuss Caleb. The following is a questionnaire we led her through to help get her unstuck and moving forward with this tough nugget.

Caleb Time

Student name: *Caleb*   Grade: *3*

List your student's strengths, positive attributes, and resiliency factors. Consider questions such as the following to prompt your summary of what makes your student awesome:

- What does this student like?
- Who are they connected to?
- What are things they are doing well?
- Where are they succeeding?

- What makes them smile and feel happy?
- What are they good at?
- What do they want to be when they grow up?
- When they are at their best, what is fun and likable about them?
- What would their family member (or someone who loves them a lot) say is great about them?
- What are some strengths you've noted about your student's family?

Caleb is quite likable and funny. He has a good sense of humor and is able to joke with adults and make things fun. He is really good at drawing and loves to doodle anime characters. He wants to be an artist and draw cartoons when he grows up. Some classmates ask him to draw their favorite characters for them, and that is a way they connect. He is most connected to our school resource officer, Mr. Rios, as they talk about motorcycles and video games together.

Caleb does best with peers when the group is small and they are doing noncompetitive things, like drawing or climbing on the playground equipment. He has two friends in class who seem to make him happy and who enjoy him. Academically, Caleb enjoys creative assignments and projects where he can draw, design, or build. If he doesn't have to write much, he will engage and can be a productive part of a group. He has mentioned possibly wanting to be a welder like his uncle.

At his best, Caleb is fun, funny, and enjoyable to be around. His family says he is sweet, a good big brother, and always tinkering and building stuff. They say he is very warm and gives incredible hugs.

- What is your goal for this student?

I want Caleb to fulfill his potential for learning. I want him to pursue interests that he's passionate about. I want him to experience joy and curiosity, to build and maintain positive connections and friendships with peers, and to develop resilience so he can remain regulated during tough times and push forward to learn important things that he is avoiding.

Now that you are in Part 2 and have addressed how you present "wonderful, beautiful you" to your setting, it's time to direct your attention outward to support your wonderful, beautiful tough nugget. At certain points where we've outlined a strategy or an insight, we include a vignette from Caleb's ongoing case study so that you can see the work in practice, and we also give you a turn to write your truth. The first Your Turn section follows.

> ### Your Turn
>
> Student name: _____
> Grade: _____
>
> List your student's strengths, positive attributes, and resiliency factors. Consider questions such as the following to prompt your summary of what makes your student awesome:
>
> What does this student like?
>
> _____
> _____
>
> Who are they connected to?
>
> _____
> _____
>
> What are things they are doing well?
>
> _____
> _____
>
> Where are they succeeding?
>
> _____
> _____

What makes them smile and feel happy?
_____
_____

What are they good at?
_____
_____

What do they want to be when they grow up?
_____
_____

When they are at their best, what is fun and likable about them?
_____
_____

What would their family member (or someone who loves them a lot) say is great about them?
_____
_____

What are some strengths you've noted about your student's family?
_____
_____

What is your goal for this student?
_____
_____

What is it like to answer these questions? Maybe you find it difficult to find the good in someone you've struggled with for so long, or perhaps it is motivating to be reminded of the goodness underneath the rough behaviors. How would your student's family members feel if they read your answers? If this were your child, how would you want the teacher to answer these questions? What emotions did you experience as you wrote about your goal for your student?

This asset-based entry can be an encouraging, revelatory way to start a discussion with your student and their family. There will be plenty of time to discuss challenges further down the road. If you don't know the answers to these questions and are unsure about your student's strengths, start digging. It is important to look at the whole child and to kick off the problem-solving process by seeing something good and decent in them.

Next, Gather Relevant Information

Before you can even consider building an intervention plan for your student, you must have as much information about them as possible. We've all been in problem-solving sessions in which competent and well-meaning educators develop an excellent plan for a student, only to have information surface afterward that would have changed the entire course of the conversation. We suggest doing as much research and fieldwork as possible *before* meeting. You can get these answers by reading through your student's files, talking with school administrators and counselors, and contacting your student's past teachers. Equally valuable is talking to key figures in the child's life, including their family, caregivers, and coaches. These individuals are a rich resource and often have different experiences with your student than you do in the classroom setting. If you omit them from this process, you'll deprive yourself of vital information that can help you help your tough nugget.

Caleb Time

Before meeting with Caleb's student support team, we asked them to do some historical research, emphasizing the importance of gathering as much information as possible about Caleb before trying to identify how to help him. As consultants, we advise staff to be as prepared as possible with knowledge about all aspects of their students, not just what they're struggling with. Ms. Coombs had already talked with the teacher who taught Caleb for half of last year, who said that generally, he was fine. Caleb didn't do much work but didn't get in much trouble, either. The school counselor called his previous school and learned that Caleb had had a behavior intervention plan that had not been put into the permanent file and sent on to the new school. She got his old plan, and they learned that his disruptive behavior was not new but had been going on for a few years.

Ms. Coombs called home to talk to Caleb's caregivers about what has been happening. His family was friendly and willing to talk and happy the school was reaching out. Last year's teacher had told the family that Caleb was doing "fine," but that confused them because he had not been doing fine in his previous school. Caleb's family wondered if his previous teacher really knew him. They are glad Ms. Coombs is reaching out.

Your Turn

Have you talked with other adults in the school about your student and how they perform outside your classroom? What have you discovered? How universal are the issues?

_____

_____

Have you talked with past teachers or schools? What have you found out? Is this a new issue or one that has been around for a while?

_____

_____

Have you spoken with other caregivers and family members about your student? Are they experiencing similar struggles, or do they have different experiences?

_____

_____

What has been effective in the past?

_____

_____

What insights or advice might they offer?

_____

_____

Is there a past 504/IEP/behavior intervention plan on file? If so, what's included in it?

_____

_____

Can you stitch together a family history? What are your student's family situation and dynamics, child welfare history, school performance, diagnosis (if any), and past resources and needs?

_____

_____

Wrapping Up and Looking Ahead

Information is gold, isn't it? Now that you've got some key information in hand, you're ready to take the next step: identifying what's getting in the way of your tough nugget's success. In Step 2, you'll identify those "complicating factors" and engage in a little introspection as you answer the question "How you doin'?"

STEP 2

Complicating Factors and "How You Doin'?"

As we mentioned in Step 1, it can be easy to focus on what's wrong with a student, why their behavior is not OK, or how they're frustrating you. However, we'd like to keep a positive spin on this investigation, so we're going to frame our approach with the question "What's getting in the way of this child's success?"

If you want your thinking to be clear and your interventions to be effective, you need to be in the right headspace. How do you get into the right mindset to explore all options and even consider your own role in the situation? It's time to dig in, roll up your sleeves, and explore the (perhaps heretofore unplumbed) depths of your own beliefs, values, ideas, and systems of meaning. All these affect how you interact with this child, how you think about this child in their absence, and how you approach various interactions. During this step, we prompt you to consider how you might be triggered by this student and encourage you to clear away anything that inhibits your ability to objectively and openly analyze the influence you have on your student's successes and struggles. It's quite possible that you are unwittingly a "complicating factor" that's impeding your student's progress. And that's OK: Once you know better, you can do better.

So... What's Getting in the Way of This Child's Success?

This can be a loaded question. For some students, there may be varied, complicated, intertwined factors involved. So this might be a tough ask, *and* it's important: In the Your Turn section on page 107, record all the ways your student is struggling and creating stress. For this to work, you need to record specific behaviors. First, let's see how Ms. Coombs responds to the same prompt.

> ### Caleb Time
>
> What's going on with Caleb? Well, he tends to mess around in class. He is in the 3rd grade but is functioning at a 1st grade level in academics, social skills, and his ability to regulate. He has some good days in which he generally goes with the flow and gets along with others, though he rarely engages in learning or produces much work. Typically, though, I have to send him out of the classroom at least once a day for being disruptive or outright defiant, and many times he just leaves the room when he feels like it and is hard to get back in. On the better days when Caleb is able to stay in class, he seems to shut down and doesn't do the work—but I mostly leave him alone since he is not a problem, and I can attend to others. I like Caleb generally, though I'm getting tired of dealing with him and am starting to become angry that he is taking learning away from his classmates.

This is the kind of description most educators give: a list of the disruptive and discouraging behaviors. That is a fine place to start, but to help Caleb be a better student, Ms. Coombs needs to be more precise about when and where the problems occur.

For example, instead of writing that Caleb is disruptive or defiant, which is too broad, she might write, "Caleb refuses to follow directions from teachers for much of the day on any task that he doesn't want to do." This is better, but still a little too vague. The next step is to drill down and consider the time, place, and conditions in which defiance occurs. His teacher might now write, "Caleb yells, screams, and disrupts class during math lessons." Very likely, Caleb also yells, screams, and disrupts during reading (and most direct lessons) and during unstructured time, too, so his teacher can go ahead and list those as well.

> **Your Turn**
>
> What's getting in the way of your student's success? (Remember, be specific.)
>
> _____
> _____
> _____
> _____

Great! Now that you have a thorough, specific list of things that are getting in the way of your student's success, you need to choose one or two to focus on to start. This is because it is not possible to solve all the issues at once. Change can be hard and take a while to enact, and aiming at too many goals draws focus and energy away from the team and the child. Remember, this first problem is not the *only* problem, and solving it doesn't mean you've reached the finish line. To narrow things down, identify a behavior that has high impact and, ideally, a short time frame to solve. For many educators, this would mean working on a distracting, disruptive, or energy-draining behavior like "blurting during instruction time." For others, it might be something like "leaving class without permission," which requires an adult to take time out of the day to chase the student around the school. By focusing on just one of these behaviors at a time, you'll make some progress in an area that really matters. This is how you can build your confidence to take on the next issue.

"How You Doin'?"

To make sure you are in the right mindset to solve these issues, check in with yourself. Now might be a good time to review some of the work you did in the exercises and Jot Your Thoughts sections in Chapter 1. Checking in with yourself will help you get into the right headspace and heartspace to honestly and productively confront your student's situation. The questions in the following Your Turn will help ground you and enhance your self-awareness.

Your Turn

What happens to you when you think of this student?
_____
_____

What do you think?
_____
_____

How do you feel?
_____
_____

What happens in your body—do you feel any anxiety, worry, sadness, or fear? If so, how does it manifest?
_____
_____

What story are you telling yourself about this student or the situation?
_____
_____

What are you afraid of?
_____
_____

What do you need at this time to focus on the needs of the student?
_____
_____

Here's what Ms. Coombs has to say about how she feels when she thinks about Caleb.

> ## Caleb Time
>
> Caleb has been tough most of the year. It has been taking a toll on me. When I think of him, I get anxious. He can be sweet, and he seems to like me when he is calm, but he can flip so easily and unpredictably that I feel like I'm walking on eggshells, constantly monitoring his mood to see if he will erupt.
>
> Sometimes I think he's just a kid and it's not his fault, while other times I get mad and think he's ruining learning for others and the rest of the class doesn't deserve this. In those moments, I get angry and protective of my other students. This stress manifests mostly in my stomach, where I feel anxious, and in my neck and head, where I tend to experience neck strain and headaches.
>
> The story I am telling myself varies, but I often tell a "villain and victim" story where Caleb is a mean kid acting out on purpose. I even sometimes go so far as to compare him to an abuser. And everyone else, including me, is his victim. This story leads to a lot of anger and hopelessness. On my better days (and his better days), I have more hope and can see that he is just a kid with a hard history who is doing his best, and I need to be the one to help him learn these important behavioral skills. I feel more hopeful when I am telling that story.
>
> I'm not sure exactly what I need to be able to focus on Caleb's needs. Sometimes I need a break from him. I need to know that I am not failing the other kids in the class. I need to know I am not the only one working to help him learn these skills. I also need some help to find time (take something off my plate maybe?) to connect better with Caleb and then give him some practice with some of his missing behavioral skills.

Wrapping Up and Looking Ahead

In our experience, in almost every setting where children and adults convene, Step 2 is the most challenging. It's a straightforward process to record the behaviors that are impeding a child's success, since they're plain to see and hear and easy to describe. Where it becomes challenging is acknowledging your emotions, your role, and your influence on the situation. If you are unaware of how this child and their attitude and behaviors are affecting you, you will react from a place of anxiety, stress, and frustration and may unwittingly become part of the problem. If your own fears and emotions are not held in check, no strategies or interventions will be successful. Be sure to spend some time exploring how you are being affected and what help you might need to become as effective as possible.

In Step 3 you'll assess the environment you establish—the culture of safety—from your student's perspective.

STEP 3
Culture of Safety

In Chapter 2, we discussed the importance of creating a culture of safety—a nest—in your classroom and school. This is imperative for all students, especially for students who come from hard places, as their stress response systems have been wired to be sensitized, and they respond to hints of threat or danger in an exaggerated way. Many students who are not feeling safe shut down or fight back—and not-so-good things ensue.

Remember, it's not just about *being* safe; you know your students are as safe as they can be in your setting. It is *feeling* safe that matters. In a broad sense, ask yourself this: To what extent do your students feel safe in your setting? How do you know? How do you measure this? (Idea: Ask your students!)

The following questions can help you view your culture of safety through the lens of your tough nugget.

 Your Turn

To what extent does your tough nugget experience *safety* in your environment? How do you know? How do you measure this? Does your tough nugget...

- Believe that you like them?

_____

_____

- Feel like they belong and have a place in the classroom?

- Believe they can be vulnerable and make mistakes?

- Have opportunities to understand and uncover their emotions?

- Have the opportunity to be themselves without being teased or bullied?

- Believe they are capable of being successful in your environment?

To what extent does your environment support regulation and safety?

- Does your tough nugget have sensory issues that get in their way of being comfortable or safe?

- Does the lighting need to be changed or do seating choices need to be offered to meet some basic physical or physiological needs?

To what extent does your tough nugget experience *predictability* in your environment? How do you know? How do you measure this?

- What visual reminders do you have of your norms, expectations, and schedule?

  _____

  _____

- Are routines and schedules established?

  _____

  _____

- When there are changes to a routine or schedule, are there prompts and reminders so students can prepare?

  _____

  _____

To what extent does your tough nugget experience *consistency* in your environment? How do you know? How do you measure this?

- Are you calm and grounded each day, so students experience you in a similar way despite your own stress level or workload?

  _____

  _____

- Do all staff members respond in consistent ways to positive as well as disruptive behaviors?

  _____

  _____

- Is there a common language for teaching and responding to misbehavior in different environments throughout the school?

  _____

  _____

Caleb Time

After answering the questions on pages 111–113, Ms. Coombs wrote the following summary.

For Caleb to feel safe, he needs a calm and predictable environment. When things are chaotic, or when he is not sure what is going on, he gets anxious and is not at his best. I know that when things get too loud or there are too many stimuli, Caleb struggles to stay focused and seems to get overwhelmed. Recently, I changed the lighting in the classroom by turning down the overhead fluorescent lights and bringing in some lamps and string lights. The room was less stark and bright, which seemed to soften the energy of the classroom.

I also continued to work on Caleb's seating so that he would not be overstimulated. I placed him on the edge and near the front, where he couldn't see his classmates as much, and I removed most of his supplies from his desk. This helped because he had fewer things to keep track of and get distracted by. In addition, he now has to ask to get his supplies. I was not a fan of this idea at first, thinking that it would be an excuse for him not to do work and that I would have to constantly get him things. Instead, I taught him how to ask for what he needed, and then I got to say "yes" to him a lot. This means he got more "yes's" during the day, which was a goal of mine (he was getting a lot of "no's" before). Also, this meant he was able to get up to get his supplies, and I knew I needed to increase the amount of physical movement he got in the day to help him stay regulated. I had to work out a system where his supplies would be in a part of the room that was easy to access, so he wouldn't have to cross in front of all the other students and get distracted or be disruptive.

I also allowed for some flexible seating options, so that Caleb, when he asked correctly, could move to the calming corner or to the soft chair near the back when he needed a break. I taught Caleb how to ask for these breaks using appropriate hand signals, and I role-played with him right and wrong ways to ask. We also practiced the skill of "accepting no" and, when no students were around, he role-played asking for some supplies (getting a yes); asking to get a calming fidget (getting a yes); and then asking to move to the soft chair (and getting a no). He then had to demonstrate his technique for handling getting a no, which was to take a deep breath and say, "OK."

I have clear expectations and group norms posted in the classroom. Caleb knows what they are, and I feel like this is a strength.

I am fairly consistent and predictable in my mood and energy, and I have established classroom routines, which is helpful. Our classroom schedule is posted, and we have routines throughout the day—same times for morning meeting, reading time, lunch, math, and so on.

I have taught the class regulation skills. The school counselor taught a "flip your lid" lesson at the beginning of the year, and I use that language consistently. I have "zones of regulation" posters and prompts visible, and we use this approach consistently throughout the school. However, I don't think I have been consistent in using this language proactively. I really only discuss regulation when students are dysregulated. I need to bring that language into daily check-ins and ask students to notice and name their regulation state consistently. Caleb needs even more practice than this, and I will need to find some other adults in the school to give him time to practice the skills—noticing his state, using the language, and asking for what he needs in the moment.

* * *

Over time, with lots of repetition, Caleb began to use his words more and ask for what he needed. Ms. Coombs kept checking in with him and, by doing so, showed great care and concern and increased her understanding of and attunement to Caleb. She began to be able to read his state and catch him before he escalated. Caleb heard more "yes's" and had some control over where he sat and moved, all of which helped him stay more regulated. At first, the bar was set low, and he was allowed to move around and stand or sit in the corner as

> long as he was not disrupting anyone else's learning. As he gained some ability to manage himself and experience some success, Caleb's student support team slowly started raising the bar by asking Caleb to get a little work done before moving or getting his "yes."

 Your Turn

What about *your* "Caleb"? Are there changes you can put in place that will help with safety and regulation, such as reconsidering their seating location? Increasing seating options? Reducing overstimulation by changing lights or minimizing clutter? Reducing understimulation by allowing for breaks and movement throughout the day? What skills are missing for your student that you can teach proactively when both you and they are calm? You might want to access your student's responses to the Safety Survey (see Figure 2.1 on p. 37) to inform your decision making.

_____
_____
_____
_____
_____
_____
_____
_____
_____

Wrapping Up and Looking Ahead

This step has given you an opportunity to focus on the all-important environment in which your tough nugget spends time every day. Safety, predictability, and consistency are foundational to supporting a student who is experiencing tough times, struggling in a setting, and needing calm, empathetic care. As the primary adult professional caregiver, you're likely to be the most attuned to your student's challenges, needs, and experience. In Step 4, we'll shift your attention to the relationships and connections that bond your tough nugget with your setting—especially your student's relationship with you.

STEP 4
Fostering Connections

Up to this point, we've discussed who your student is, what's getting in the way of their learning, and how you can create a safe nest conducive to learning. Now it's time to talk relationships. What is your relationship with your student like? Do you feel connected to each other? Are you able to find things about this child to like and appreciate? Do they feel seen, heard, and valued in your class? If this student is indeed a tough nugget, there will be some conflicts. Are you committed to repair and reset? Can you successfully put a repair in place that conveys your genuine commitment to resetting to connection—meaning that you are prioritizing the relationship and are ready to move forward in partnership? These are hard questions, and the tougher the nugget, the harder they are to answer. However, they are critical to your success moving forward.

Caleb Time

We asked Ms. Coombs to reflect on her relationship with Caleb, giving her the following prompts.

- What is your relationship with this student? *Strained, really. Sometimes good, but often rough.*
- When were you last in sync? Is there something specific to which you can attribute that rapport? *It has been a while. We have had some good days, but I don't know what is different about those days. I need to think on this more.*

- When did you last experience a rift? What, specifically, caused it? *Every day, it seems. Mostly me pushing him to do things he doesn't want to do or telling him to stop distracting others.*
- On a scale of 1–10, how much do you like and respect this student? *I vacillate between 4 and 8. Sometimes I enjoy Caleb and can see the sweet boy inside. Sometimes I resent him and have a hard time seeing his strengths.*
- On a scale of 1–10, how much would this student say you like and respect them? *Unsure. I guess I have to ask?*
- On a scale of 1–10, how much does this student like and respect you? *Same.*

Ms. Coombs followed up her answers to the questions with further reflection.

So, generally speaking, on good days I like Caleb, and it seems as if he likes me. However, he doesn't have many good days, so most of the time I find myself not liking him a lot.

It felt weird to ask Caleb how he feels about me, but I found a calm time and asked him honestly, does he like me and does he think that I like him? He said that, in general, he likes me but feels like I'm always on his back and he is in trouble all the time. He said that sometimes when other kids do things, I am nicer to them and they don't get in trouble, so that doesn't seem fair. He also said that sometimes he quits trying to listen to me because it doesn't seem to matter—that he can have a good morning and be trying hard and it doesn't seem like I even notice.

While he was talking, I tried to simply listen and reflect; I did not try to shift his perspective or explain my point of view until the very end. I thanked him for his honesty and willingness to let me know how he was feeling. I acknowledged his point of view as much as possible and said that it probably did feel at times like I was on his back and that I am less hard on some of the other students. At the end, when I was confident that he felt heard and his lid was on, I did tell him a little bit about what I need from him and why I might respond differently to him than some other students, but I kept it short.

> *The simple act of having this conversation seemed to help us both. Caleb appeared to feel a bit closer, safer, and less reactive with me. For my part, I recognized that I was being harsh with him and that he needed more encouragement. I set a goal to catch him being good and notice and praise the times when he was not being disruptive rather than ignore it and hope he would continue behaving on his own.*

Now reflect on your relationship with your student in the following Your Turn section.

Your Turn

What is your relationship with this student?

_____
_____

When were you last in sync? Is there something specific to which you can attribute that rapport?

_____
_____

When did you last experience a rift? What, specifically, caused it?

_____
_____

On a scale of 1–10, how much do you like and respect this student? (*Note:* If your number is 7 or below, revisit Step 1. If that doesn't help you see your student in a warmer, more human way, poll some colleagues and find some things to like and appreciate about your kiddo.)

_____

_____

On a scale of 1–10, how much would this student say you like and respect them? (*Note:* Even if you are working to find things to like about your student, if they don't feel it or believe it, you will need to do more work here. Some students take a long time to get through to, so keep sending the message that you are on their side.)

_____

_____

On a scale of 1–10, how much does this student like and respect you? (*Note:* This is another indicator of relationship, and if the score is 7 or below, you will need to start here.)

_____

_____

Relationship *has* to be at the forefront. If any of these questions gets a score of 7 or below, you must stop working on problem solving, goal setting, and behavior change and refocus on relationship building and safety.

With this reflection exercise, our goal has been to help you work on the one area you have control over: yourself! If you have the right mindset and are actively working toward liking your student; noticing their strengths; and believing they are decent, good, and worthy (despite tough behaviors), then you are doing the most important work.

6 Connection Strategies

Now let's consider other ways you can continue to build a relationship with your tough nugget. When you read and processed our list of top 10 proactive relationship-building strategies in Chapter 3 (pp. 45–47), you likely recognized some of the approaches and hopefully added a few to your tool kit.

Working with a tough nugget, though, is different than casting a wide net to try to foster connections with everyone. The following are strategies we share with teachers when they feel like they are not connecting with a student. Which ones might work with your tough nugget?

But first, two words of advice: Practice empathy. Try to view things through the lens of how your tough nugget is experiencing them, rather than simply what you are doing.

1. Use special greetings. As an extension of the "hugs, high fives, and handshakes" strategy from Chapter 3 (p. 46), you can make a special point to greet your tough nugget at the door, in the bus line, on the playground, and during in-class transitions. Maybe you can even work together to come up with a special greeting ritual. This practice will increase connection and decrease misbehavior, helping your student to feel seen and noticed in a positive way.

2. Check in often. You have many, many opportunities during the school day to check in with your tough nugget. Stop by their desk for a 30-second check-in; offer an extended welcome after transitions; ask about their family, pet, hobby, or interest; or simply kneel next to them while they're working and ask if they need help or have questions. These are all ways to communicate "I see you."

3. Try 2x10. We briefly mentioned the 2x10 strategy in Chapter 3. To try it, simply carve out two minutes of special time daily to connect with your tough nugget for 10 consecutive days. In each two-minute window, you can share a joke, ask questions, play a quick game, work on a task together, share a bite to eat, or express curiosity about what your student is interested in. By doing so, you'll build trust and demonstrate consistent caring. Plus, you'll learn some information about your tough nugget that you can use later!

4. Catch 'em being good. This is classic parenting advice and crucial for building trust and relationship. Just as you'll see misbehavior if you're looking for it, you'll also see awesomeness if you keep your eyes open. Follow up your positive observations with encouraging feedback and praise. Whether you subscribe to the 4:1, 5:1, or

10:1 positive-to-negative interaction ratio philosophy (see the following strategy), the point is to inundate your tough nugget with positivity and promote moments of success, cooperation, engagement, and participation. Lots of them.

5. Maintain a 5:1 positivity-to-negativity ratio. As we just mentioned, it can be helpful to precipitate an abundance of positive interactions. Remain keen to the positives (smiles, encouragement, praise, eye contact, celebrations, and yes's) and the negatives (frowns, corrections, disregard, turning away, punishments, and no's), and try to ensure the former outweigh the latter. A 5:1 ratio is ideal. You may be surprised to notice that your feedback tends to reflect what's actually happening in the classroom; that is, if the student is misbehaving 80 percent of the time, about 80 percent of your feedback will be corrective, or negative. Shifting the balance of your interactions can help shift your student's behaviors, too.

6. Always repair. We discussed the practice of repair in Chapter 3, and it's a vital strategy to employ with your tough nugget. Most likely, you'll experience quite a few incidents and rifts with your student, and each time you'll have a choice: Sweep it under the rug or confront it via repair. We advocate for repair, every time. These discussions demonstrate your willingness to make the relationship and the school experience better for your student, which builds trust and connection.

What's the big idea with these strategies? Actually, there are two. First, your tough nugget is going to need something different, something more, something special to trust and connect with you enough to forge a strong, enduring relationship. Second, if you drill into your mind that you are your tough nugget's champion, every approach and interaction you have with them will change for the better.

 Your Turn

Which of the six strategies are you willing to employ?

Why do you think it will be successful?

_____

_____

What is your ratio of positive to negative interactions with your tough nugget?

_____

_____

Commit to using one of the strategies for two weeks. Much like a 2x10, if you apply it with consistent effort, you're likely to see results. Keep some anecdotal notes on your progress in Figure S4.1.

Figure S4.1 Notes on Strategy Progress

Strategy selected: _____

Date	Notes on Student's Response to the Strategy

Caleb Time

I recognize that Caleb needs more encouragement and praise from me, so I initiated a repair by telling him that I have been thinking a lot about how he feels like he is always in trouble. I reassured him that I do like him and enjoy having him in class, and I apologized for not conveying that message to him more regularly. I told him I wanted him to feel safe and that he could talk with me, so I set a time twice a week to talk one-on-one. At first, we talked about school stuff, but then I tried to discuss things outside school that were interesting to him. Slowly, we got to know each other better, and that connection time helped us both be less reactive to each other and have more grace.

During these discussions, I learned that Caleb doesn't really like to be praised in front of everyone. He doesn't like being called out or feeling different, even if it's for a good thing. I learned that when he is doing well, it works better to move near him and give him a touch on the shoulder and a smile and a thanks. I have also begun writing quick notes on stickies and putting them on his desk. He seems to like that.

Caleb already had a good relationship with the school resource officer, Mr. Rios, so we asked him if he'd be willing to serve as Caleb's champion. Instead of just being welcoming and friendly when Caleb is in trouble, Mr. Rios has been making an effort to find Caleb every day, even if just to check in and ask how life is going. He asks questions but avoids focusing on Caleb's academic or behavioral performance, instead talking about life, family, dreams, games, and anything else of interest. His job is to help Caleb feel seen, heard, valued, and special. Mr. Rios is doing a great job with this, and the effort seems to be paying off, as Caleb is showing more connection to school, is absent a little less often, and seems to enjoy being here more.

Your Turn

How does your tough nugget like to be praised?
_____
_____

Are you noticing when your student is doing well, even when the positive behavior is small or expected?
_____
_____

Does your student have a champion?
_____
_____

With whom does your student tend to interact positively?
_____
_____

How could you determine which adults are in a position of trust and connection with your student?
_____
_____

What steps could you take to find a suitable champion for your student?
_____
_____

What does your student have to say about the adults in their orbit?
_____
_____

Peer Relationships

It is through the power of your relationship that you have the most influence on a student. The adult in the room is not the only important relationship, however, and the older students get, the truer that becomes. Developing and nurturing peer relationships can help students get their needs met and take the pressure off adults to meet all of a student's connection needs.

> ### Caleb Time
>
> Caleb has a couple of peers he is connected to. I have tried to create groups and teams that forced students to work with different peers, but that doesn't always work great. I know I need to continue to find time to teach teamwork as a skill, which is important for all students. I am very mindful of who can sit next to Caleb and who I can pair him with. I am trying two things. First, I am talking to the peers who can handle Caleb. I pulled them aside and asked for their help, telling them that Caleb needed some peers to play with him and encourage him. I pointed out their strengths and wondered if they could use their skills to help Caleb feel more connected. They are doing a good job trying to encourage him and include him. I can see that it isn't always easy, and they need support, especially at the times when Caleb is not kind or rejects them. I have found a couple of times to coach them in ways they can respond and how they can look at his behavior in a way where they don't take it personally. I continue to remind them about the zones of regulation and how the dysregulated brain can struggle with accessing helpful, healthy, and safe choices. I assure them that Caleb isn't being a bad person when he says hurtful things and that sometimes when our brains are dysregulated, we say and do things that can hurt others. I am working with them on having Caleb repair with his teammates when he does make those choices and modeling the power of giving grace, as none of us is perfect.

> So far this seems to be helping, as Caleb has a little more connection and grace, and it is good for his peers too, as they get to practice skills and develop and demonstrate real empathy. I am worried, though, that I will need to switch mentor peers soon, as it is not fair to these students to have that responsibility for too long, and the pool of calm and helpful students is small. It will be a challenge to find and then train and coach new peer mentors.
>
> The student support team also suggested that we find a way for Caleb to be a mentor. We started pairing him up with a couple of 1st grade boys who need extra attention and support. We sometimes have Caleb read to them, coach them in math, and give them some extra exercise when needed by running around the yard. The first couple of times, it went really well, and Caleb seemed to love feeling smart and having students look up to him. However, he is at their developmental level and things can devolve quickly, so we need to monitor closely to make sure he is doing OK.

Your Turn

To what extent does your student connect with peers?
_____
_____

Does your tough nugget work well with others?
_____
_____

Who are your student's friends?
_____
_____

When other students talk with your tough nugget, do they use their name?
_____
_____

To what extent is your student included in activities, group projects, stories, jokes, special events, and other opportunities for peers to gather?
_____
_____

What windows are open for you to enlist the efforts of peers to include your tough nugget?
_____
_____

What opportunities do you have to partner your tough nugget with a younger student to be a mentor, or an older student to have a "big buddy" of some kind?
_____
_____

How might your student offer a service to the school or community using their skills, talents, or tools?
_____
_____

How could these approaches change the way your student's classmates receive and interact with them?
_____
_____

Wrapping Up and Looking Ahead

Relationships are very important. Clearly, we believe this to be the case, as we prioritize them throughout this workbook. They're not a panacea, however; the way forward is truly a blend of all these steps, approaches, mindsets, and tools. As you continue to get a deeper grasp on what's going on with your tough nugget, you will refine your course of action. In Step 5, we'll walk you through the process of identifying whether the behaviors you're seeing are a matter of will… or a matter of skill.

STEP 5

Won't...or Can't?

We have established that helping students who are struggling begins with creating a sense of safety. When students feel calm, relaxed, and safe, they tend to do better. Lots of things can make a student feel unsafe during the school day, and many of them we cannot control. What we *do* have control over is... wait for it... ourselves. Remember Exercise 3 in Chapter 1 (p. 21)? You can control your actions, reactions, words, voice tone, and thoughts, the last of which include the stories you tell yourself about your tough nuggets.

That's right: The stories you tell yourself are profound and can change not just your attitude and your sense of safety, but also your experience, which in turn can significantly influence the type of environment you are creating for your students. So wouldn't it be helpful to be mindful of the stories you tell yourself about students who struggle? We call these mind shifts *reframes* because by shifting your story or frame of reference just a little, you can find yourself feeling calmer and more empathetic, patient, and resilient. In this chapter, we look at the three most powerful reframes that resilient educators use. (We introduced these reframes as key ideas in Chapter 4, so return to pp. 58–63 for more background.)

Reframe #1: It's Not About You

Remember, the behaviors of students who experience numerous not-OK things or who come from hard places are most often efforts to self-regulate, to seek the feeling of safety, or to satisfy an unmet need. They've got stuff they're working on and dealing with. It's not about you. Behaviors that feel comfortable to these students aren't necessarily healthy; many of our tough nuggets have not learned effective ways to manage their emotions and experiences. They are doing the best they can with what they have in the moment.

So, start here by saying, "It's not about me!" Repeat this phrase whenever you need a reminder; it has power!

> ### Caleb Time
>
> Caleb disrupts class often, either making noise or wandering around and refusing to be in his seat. ("Something is going on with him, and... it's not about me.")
>
> If he is playing a game and I ask him to stop and transition, he will ignore me and not move a muscle, as if I'm not there. ("That is frustrating and feels disrespectful, and... it's not about me.")
>
> When we are working on math, he'll crumple up his paper and say, "This is stupid, I don't need to know it." ("This is a button for me, and... it's not about me.")

Your Turn

List the challenging attitude and behaviors of your tough nugget here:

_____
_____
_____
_____

Now, read each challenging behavior you've listed and say, "It's not about me." This exercise is even more powerful if you sit with each one for a moment. Imagine the behavior. Visualize the situation and the emotions involved. Put yourself in that place and feel the pressure of the moment. Now that you are there, say aloud, "It's not about me."

We'll help you uncover what is prompting the behaviors of your tough nugget in Step 6. In the meantime, consider the following exercise.

> **Your Turn**
>
> How does it feel to know it's not about you? For many, it is relieving, freeing, and calming.
>
> _____
>
> _____
>
> Does this practice support your self-regulation?
>
> _____
>
> _____
>
> Are there times when it is easier not to take it personally? When would that be? Are there times when it is harder? What do those look like?
>
> _____
>
> _____
>
> What else can you do to remind yourself that the behavior in front of you is not about you?
>
> _____
>
> _____

Very rarely do students misbehave deliberately to ruin an educator's day (or life). Most of the time, students are simply reacting from their own histories and insecurities, and it has nothing to do with you. If you are a safe enough, healthy enough person in their lives, some students will feel more comfortable putting their emotions on display, and it may feel like they're taking it out on you. In fact, you may be the safe person for them to really let you know how *not OK* their life is! In the cases where the behavior *does* have something to do with you, it could be that you haven't yet established a culture of safety or a strong enough connection with them and they do not trust you or want to work with you—they may even fear you. If you find you still have work to do to build a safe nest and a solid relationship, go ahead and revisit Steps 3 and 4.

Your Turn

Go back to your list of challenging behaviors (p. 132) and consider the following questions.

Are any of your reactions to these behaviors about you? Are you being triggered because of your own history or insecurities?

_____

_____

You answered the following questions in Exercise 2 (p. 19). Hopefully that exercise helped you get a better understanding of yourself and your buttons. Now go through the activity again, specifically with your tough nugget in mind.

When was the last time I flipped my lid for reasons related to my tough nugget?

_____

_____

_____

_____

What behavior pushed my button?

_____

_____

_____

STEP 5. WON'T... OR CAN'T?

___

What is the button? Why is that a button for me?

___

What can I do to make that button less sensitive?

___

Caleb Time

Ms. Coombs reflected on the prompts we provided.

Incident: Caleb, for the fourth time that day, started bothering his peers while they worked. When I reminded him, he yelled and swore at me. I called for behavioral support and the school counselor came and removed him from class for a while.

Button: I am working so hard to help my students, and when Caleb is disruptive, I get angry. There is righteous anger because I think it is unfair that he hurts the other students by disrupting their learning. Behind the anger is

> also worry and fear. I worry that our scores will be low, and it will reflect badly on me. I am concerned that his behavior will be seen as "normal" or acceptable in some way and other students will mimic him. In those moments I also feel afraid of losing control. I feel powerless in that moment to affect something so important to me, and I hate that feeling.
>
> Why is that a button for me? I grew up in a family where hard work and achievement were emphasized. I know I am loved, but I also carry the "you must be perfect" rock in my backpack, and when Caleb acts out, I feel out of control and like I am failing, and I really struggle anytime I am not performing well.
>
> During those moments, I need to remember that Caleb has his own history and has many unmet needs (most of which are due to things beyond my control). I need to remind myself that there is so much I can do to meet his needs while he's with me and to reassure myself that my being a safe, predictable, and consistent support can make a difference for him in the long run. I can stay calm in the moment if I
>
> - Am aware of my button and can catch the trigger early.
> - Tell myself, "It is not about me."
> - Tell myself that Caleb is just doing what he knows and has been taught and that he is doing his best with what he's got.
> - Remind myself that what Caleb needs are thousands of repetitions of warm, caring responses from regulated adults. I can give him as many as I can, but it is not all on me to fix the problem. I need to rely on and trust the larger system to help him grow.

Reframe #2: Behavior Is Communication

Most student behavior follows a predictable pattern that is generally easy for adults to understand. Some students, based on their biology, history, attachment issues, or other factors, present strange or confusing behaviors. It's important to remember that those behaviors are students' attempts to get their needs met. When adults understand this, they tend to be less triggered by a student's behaviors and more curious, wondering what the student is communicating and what need they are trying to meet or problem they are trying to solve.

As students get older, they tend to be better at using their words to communicate, though this is not always the case. The more stressed or dysregulated they get, the fewer words they will use. Sometimes by shutting down and refusing to work, a student is making one or more of the following statements:

- "This is too hard for me."
- "I don't know where to start."
- "I don't feel safe trying."
- "I need help, but I don't know how to ask (or I'm embarrassed to ask)."
- "Compared with other things in my life, this is not important to me right now."
- "I need help understanding these complicated concepts."

When a student is angry and defiant, they could be trying to tell you the following:

- "I'm overwhelmed and need help controlling myself."
- "I don't know what else to do to be heard."
- "I want to do well, but I have no idea how."
- "I am filled with big emotions, and I don't know how to express or manage them appropriately."
- "I need help understanding these complicated emotions."

And sometimes when a student is struggling with peers, they are communicating the following:

- "I want to have friends, but I don't know how to make them."
- "I feel alone and rejected, and it makes me angry."
- "No one likes me, and it makes me feel upset, so I make others feel upset."
- "The only way I know how to get attention is by making inappropriate comments."
- "I need help understanding these complicated relationships."

Caleb Time

We asked Ms. Coombs to list some of Caleb's behaviors that bothered her and to consider what he might be communicating through them. The table in Figure S5.1 shows the results of her reflection.

Figure S5.1 What Caleb's Behavior Might Be Communicating

Behavior	Possible Communication
Disrupting class: blurting things out and wandering the class disturbing others	"I can't control myself. I need to be taught and practice ways to deal with my impulsivity." "I feel insecure about my friends and don't know how to get their attention appropriately. I need to be taught how to do that." "I struggle to believe I can get my needs met if I lose the attention of the adult. I need to be seen constantly, or I get anxious." "I need to be seen, so I do what I can to get reassurance that I am important, even if it means getting in trouble."
Ignoring directions/ refusing to comply	"I don't like being asked to do something I don't want to do. If I don't want to do it, I refuse, and I like feeling that I am in control. When I get my way, I feel better." "I hate changing. I want to stay where I feel good and safe and doing what I like." "When I feel worried, anxious, or fearful, I try to control anything that I can, which means if you tell me to do something, I automatically jump to fighting it. I need to feel like it is my choice or I have some power."
Walking away, shutting down, and not doing anything	"I hate feeling stupid or standing out, so I would rather not do it than risk failing in front of others." "I do want to be successful, but I've failed time and time again, so why should I try?" "This stuff does not seem important to me at all, and working on it makes me feel lousy and lose control. I don't like losing control."

Your Turn

What about your tough nugget? List a few of their behaviors in Figure S5.2 and what they might be communicating to you.

Figure S5.2 What Your Student's Behavior Might Be Communicating

Behavior	Possible Communication

What was this activity like for you?

_____

_____

Are you able to dig deep and put yourself in your tough nugget's shoes to see what might be behind the behavior?

_____

_____

How does this change how you view your student's behaviors?

_____

_____

> *Note:* This takes practice. If you get stuck, you can consult with a friend or colleague who is especially good at staying calm and enjoying even the most challenging kids. Ask them, "How do you remain calm in the storm?" Record their responses and keep a running list of reframes that are most helpful for you here.
>
> _____
>
> _____
>
> _____
>
> _____

Reframe #3: Won't... or Can't?

When we grasp how stress and trauma affect not only the brain's chemical reactions but also its wiring (neuron connections), we understand that some students come to school incapable of doing some of the thinking, problem solving, and regulating that is expected of kids their age.

The moment your student falls short of expectations, you have a decision to make—a story to tell. One story is that your student (or colleague or family member, to extend this practice) *won't* do what you are asking. Telling this story means you believe that your student is consciously deciding to defy, ignore, or disregard you—which usually leads to some angst and irritation, followed by your reaction, which is typically designed to increase the student's motivation so that they will meet your expectations. This motivational strategy can vary, but it often incorporates some positive reinforcement and much more negative reinforcement.

The reality is that all of us need motivation and incentive to do things, especially things that are not our preferred activities. However, if a student is *unable* to do a task, then all the motivational strategies in the world will not help at that moment. Imagine how frustrating it would be to face a challenge you know you cannot do (for example, replacing the engine in your car with no knowledge of automotive repair) while being bombarded with even the best-intentioned cheerleading, encouragement, and appeals to "just try harder!"

We advise making this fundamental assumption about students: *They would be successful if they could.* We believe that all students want to succeed, and if they are not succeeding, it is because of an unmet need or an undeveloped ability—or what Dr. Ross Greene (2009) refers to as "lagging skills."

Figure S5.3 shows a list of skills, divided into four categories, that are crucial for students to develop to thrive in school and beyond. Read through the list of skills and put a checkmark next to any that you believe your student is lagging in. Note that this is a short list. To be successful in school and navigate this complex world requires so many tangible and intangible skills that it would be impossible to list them all.

Figure S5.3 Checklist of Skills Students Need to Succeed

✓	Academic	✓	Social
	Reading		Empathy and compassion
	Processing speed (verbal or written)		Understanding other perspectives
	Math computation		Reading social cues
	Writing proficiency		Conflict resolution
✓	**Executive Functioning**		Self-advocacy/getting needs met
	Working memory		Negotiating needs
	Task initiation		Friendship/social skills
	Planning	✓	**Personal**
	Organization		Self-awareness
	Inhibitory/impulse control		Identifying emotions
	Flexibility		Regulation skills
	Study skills		Stop and think
	Time management		Linking actions to consequences
	Sustained attention		Delayed gratification and patience
	Transitioning activities or attention		Self-initiation skills

Caleb Time

Figure S5.4 shows Ms. Coombs's filled-in chart listing possible skills in further need of development that could explain Caleb's behaviors.

Figure S5.4 Caleb's Behaviors and Skills in Possible Need of Development

Behavior	Skill in Possible Need of Development
Disrupting class: blurting things out and wandering the class disturbing others	• Needs self-awareness and regulation skills • Needs impulse control and to understand "stop and think" • Needs to connect actions to consequences • Needs to understand and be able to ask for what he needs/self-advocate
Ignoring directions/refusing to comply	• Needs self-awareness and regulation skills • Needs ability to transition from one activity to another • Needs practice following directions and "accepting no"
Walking away, shutting down, and not doing anything	• Needs self-awareness and regulation skills • Needs practice identifying emotions • Needs awareness of needs and practice negotiating needs • Needs to build confidence and self-efficacy

Your Turn

How about your tough nugget? When they fail to meet expectations, is it because they don't want to, or because they are not able to? Have you tried multiple motivational strategies without success? That is often the sign that your student *can't* meet the expectation for some reason, not that they *won't*. If you were to look at it through that lens, what undeveloped skill might be getting in the way of your student's success? Fill in the blank template in Figure S5.5.

Figure S5.5 Your Student's Behaviors and Skills in Possible Need of Development

Behavior	Skill in Possible Need of Development

What do you notice/wonder?
_____
_____

How does this information give you a new view of your tough nugget's behaviors?
_____
_____

How does this information give you a new view of your tough nugget's needs?
_____
_____

How does this information give you a new view of your tough nugget's undeveloped skill(s)?
_____
_____

Wrapping Up and Looking Ahead

Often, we attribute student "misbehaviors" to willful disobedience—the intent to cause mischief, disrupt class, or defy us on purpose. The reality is much more complex: Students may behave in certain ways because they've not yet developed or refined the skills necessary to meet academic, environmental, interpersonal, or other expectations. In Step 6, you'll see how students' unmet needs drive their behaviors—and you'll get a chance to "needsleuth" your tough nugget to unpack what's going on at the heart of the matter.

STEP 6

Needsleuthing

In Step 6, we place the spotlight fully on your student. As we've established, kids have needs that must be met before they can be learning-ready, so in this step, we walk you through a thorough exploration of your student's needs. There are four major categories of need (previously described in Chapter 4) that often go unmet, and it's likely that your student's needs are confusingly distributed across multiple categories. That's OK—we'll help you funnel the list to prioritize the most pressing, distracting need first.

This step might take some time. What you thought you knew about your student might not be entirely accurate, so you may have to do some more observing, listening, and data gathering to help you answer our questions. Put on your needsleuthing hat and dive in!

Checking in on the 10 Factors for a Strong Brain

It can be valuable to take the time here to go back to the 10 factors for a healthy, successful brain discussed in Chapter 5 (see pp. 65–67) and assess how well your tough nugget is engaging in those on a regular basis. Any gaps or inconsistencies may account for the lack of regulation and unhelpful, unhealthy, and unsafe choices your student is making.

Needsleuthing: Peeling Back the Layers of the Artichoke

Use this process to help you identify your student's most pressing unmet need. The artichoke is a metaphor: The outer leaves are what you see (the behavior); the inner leaves are where the behavior stems from (the function, or reason for the behavior); and the heart constitutes the unmet needs that drive the behavior. Peel back the layers, identify the primary function of the behavior, and then make a case for each of the unmet needs that might be driving the behavior.

Layer 1: The Outer Leaves

This is the initial observation stage, where you pinpoint the behaviors the student is presenting. Don't try to analyze them yet; simply watch, listen, and make notes. These behaviors are how your student is showing you their *not-OK*.

Caleb Time

Ms. Coombs observed Caleb closely during this stage and jotted down her notes about two of his behaviors in a chart created for this purpose (see Figure S6.1).

Figure S6.1 Peeling Back the Outer Leaves: Caleb's Behavior

Describe the behavior here. What is happening? Be specific.		
During unpreferred activities like math and writing, Caleb will disrupt class. He will blurt things out or raise his hand and say something distracting and off topic, or he will simply get up and wander around the class and bother others.		
Frequency. How often does the behavior occur? *Two to six times a day*	**Intensity.** How severe and/or disruptive is the behavior? *Sometimes it is fairly low, like a 3/10, but can be as high as a 7/10. Usually, he leaves the class or is escorted out before we have to clear the classroom.*	**Duration.** How long do the behavioral episodes last? *The lower-level ones can last a few minutes; sometimes we lose him for more than an hour.*
Describe the behavior here. What is happening? Be specific.		
When asked to follow adults' instructions, Caleb shuts down, refuses to comply, and disregards all interaction and direction.		
Frequency. How often does the behavior occur? *Two to eight times a day*	**Intensity.** How severe and/or disruptive is the behavior? *This is less disruptive since he simply shuts down, and we often leave him alone to work it out. 3–4/10*	**Duration.** How long do the behavioral episodes last? *5–15 minutes*

Your Turn

Identify and record in Figure S6.2 the behavior that you find most distressing, disruptive, and unhealthy in your tough nugget. Be clear about what the behavior is and how and when you observe it.

Figure S6.2 Peeling Back the Outer Leaves: Your Student's Behavior

Describe the behavior here. What is happening? Be specific.		
Frequency. How often does the behavior occur?	Intensity. How severe and/or disruptive is the behavior?	Duration. How long do the behavioral episodes last?

Layer 2: The Inner Leaves

Now it's time to identify the possible functions (or reasons) for the behavior. According to applied behavior analysis (ABA),[1] (Madden, 2013), the four functions that typically prompt behavior are as follows:

---

[1] If you've been trained in how to administer a functional behavioral assessment through ABA, use that knowledge and process. If not, no worries: Use the protocol and prompts we provide to guide your investigation. Recruit the support and input of fellow educators, counselors, prior teachers, administrators, parents, guardians, and the student themselves to capture a detailed picture of what's going on and why it's happening.

1. Escape/avoidance
2. Attention seeking
3. Tangible token
4. Sensory needs

Read on for a brief overview of these four functions.

1. Escape/avoidance. Escape/avoidance is the child's attempt to get out of doing something they don't want to do. The behavior stemming from this function would typically look like running out of class, hiding under a table, losing pencils or other materials, or leaving class to go to the bathroom.

2. Attention seeking. This is the child's attempt to get the attention of adults or peers and typically presents as behaviors like acting silly, throwing a tantrum, misbehaving, and saying "no" to adults.

3. Tangible token. This function is the child's attempt to get something or do something that they enjoy. The behavior this results in might be grabbing an item from someone else, cutting in line, or crying for a toy.

4. Sensory needs (stimulation or avoidance). Sensory stimulation is the child's attempt to do something that feels good or provides a sensation. This typically would look like wiggling, bouncing, playing with their hair, biting their fingernails, or running around. Sensory avoidance is the student's effort to stay away from certain things that they find extremely distressing (Griffin et al., 2022). Behaviors stemming from sensory avoidance can include covering the head, eyes, and ears with a hoodie; walking on tiptoes; avoiding certain fabrics or foods; panicking during a fire alarm or other loud, chaotic event; hiding under their desk during unstructured classroom time; and avoiding overstimulating places or activities.

Before you begin the process of digging into the inner layers, keep in mind that a given behavior doesn't always have a specific antecedent. Sometimes a student has simply run out of the stamina necessary to manage their stress and reached a tipping point. So be careful: There may not be a predictable trigger, and it's important to stay open to the possibility that the behavior isn't a direct result of a particular incident.

Caleb Time

Figure S6.3 shows Ms. Coombs's filled-in "inner leaves" analysis chart for Caleb.

Figure S6.3 Analyzing the Inner Leaves: Caleb

Behavior. What is the behavior observed?	
Disrupting class during unpreferred activities	
Antecedent. What precipitates the behavior?	Consequence. What happens after the behavior?
Math time—once the lesson is done and it is time to get started practicing problems	• *An adult (usually me, sometimes my teaching assistant) prompts Caleb to get started.* • *If C. escalates, the adult will come to him more quickly to calm him.* • *If C. leaves the room, an adult will follow and keep eyes on him. Often, he gets to calm down with the secretaries in the office.* • *Often we will keep the same assignment so he is not left on the hook, but sometimes there is not time and we move on with the day.* • *In the office, C. gets some attention and sometimes snacks or activities to calm him.* • *We try to ignore as much behavior as we can, and sometimes this works—C. eventually complies on his own.*

Your Turn

Now it's your turn to analyze the "inner leaves" of your own student in Figure S6.4. For the identified behavior, note what prompts the behavior (the antecedent) and the result of the behavior (the consequence).

Figure S6.4 Analyzing the Inner Leaves: Your Student

Behavior. What is the behavior observed?	
Antecedent. What precipitates the behavior?	Consequence. What happens after the behavior?

Look for patterns in the behavior. Again, recruit the support and input of fellow educators, counselors, prior teachers, administrators, parents, and guardians to capture a detailed picture of what's going on and why. The following questions may help:

Are there times when or places where the behavior occurs more frequently?

_____

_____

Are there times when or places where the behavior never occurs?

_____

_____

Does the behavior occur (or not occur) around certain people?

_____

_____

> (Considering escape/avoidance in particular) Does the behavior enable the student to postpone or avoid a demanding task or get out of an unwanted situation or interaction? To what extent do you observe this?
>
> _____
>
> _____
>
> (Considering attention seeking in particular) Does the behavior enable the student to gain peer or adult attention? To what extent do you observe this?
>
> _____
>
> _____
>
> (Considering tangible token in particular) Does the behavior enable the student to gain a preferred activity or item, such as a game or toy? To what extent do you observe this?
>
> _____
>
> _____
>
> (Considering sensory stimulation or avoidance in particular) Does the behavior provide positive stimulation or avoidance of unpleasant stimulation as an alternative to the student's lack of engagement in activities? To what extent do you observe this?
>
> _____
>
> _____

Phew! That was a lot, wasn't it? You're almost ready to construct a plan to support your student—almost. You and your trusted partners have worked very hard to figure out what makes your tough nugget so tough. Before you move on to the next layer, though, pause and *talk to the student*.

We have been in hundreds of multitiered system of supports (MTSS)/problem-solving team meetings and seen so many hard-working and well-meaning adults discuss their best ideas, devise their hopeful plans, and then implement their plans with varying degrees of success. This excellent and noble work is often missing a critical piece: the student. Solving problems *for* people is almost never as powerful and effective as solving problems *with* people, no matter their age. This is as true for our youngest students as it is for adults. If you really want to know what is going on with a student and what will work best for them, you will need to ask them.

You might be thinking that if the student had any idea how to solve this problem they would have already, right? Not exactly. Although they can lend powerful insight into which needs they're trying to meet through their behavior, they need help organizing their thoughts. This is where you come in—but it's important to be patient. These students have been asked thousands of times what is going on, why they are acting this way, and what they need. They often answer these questions with shrugs and an "I don't know." The reality is, they often *don't* know or haven't yet developed the skills to accurately explain what is going on for them. Given enough time, with the support of caring adults, they can often offer crucial observations.

To get started, simply bring up the issue to the student and ask what they think is happening. For example, you might point out to the student that you have observed they are having trouble on the playground, and you wonder what is causing the problem. If they get defensive or give you an excuse or a rationale that is not tenable ("Jasmine won't leave me alone"), stay calm and again point out facts: "This occurs every day, whether Jasmine is around or not." Then ask, "What do you think is happening?" You might need to continue to repeat the process. If you are genuinely trying to hear the student's perspective (as opposed to trying to change their behavior), then the student will likely sense that and might just let their guard down and give you some insight into what is happening.

Your Turn

Based on the totality of your observations, notes, interviews, and discussions, which of the four functions do you believe is propelling this particular behavior?

1. Escape/avoidance
2. Attention seeking

3. Tangible token
4. Sensory needs

Why do you think this is the primary function behind the behavior? What have you directly observed, what evidence have you collected, and what else makes you think this is the function driving the behavior?

_____

_____

_____

Layer 3: The Heart

We have reached the final layer. It's time to determine which need is the ultimate driver of your student's behavior. First, we'll ask you to create a hypothesis for each of the four major needs (physical, emotional, relational, control), arguing that this need is the one behind the function you identified as the primary propellant of the behavior. (For a refresher on these, you may want to go back to Chapter 4; see pp. 59–60.) You're going to build four cases, trying your hardest to remain objective and open to the possibility that each case could, indeed, be the driver for this particular behavior. By putting forth all four cases, you're helping to avoid *confirmation bias*—the tendency to collect evidence and analyze it in a way that supports one's preexisting beliefs. This will ensure that you see things as they are, not as you think they are.

Physical need. Could the student have an unmet physical need that serves as the catalyst for this function? What might it be?

- How would this unmet need contribute to this particular behavior?
- How certain are you that this is the case?
- What evidence do you have that supports this hypothesis?
- What other information do you need to gather?
- Whom might you consult to collect information about your student and their needs?
- What questions do you still have?

Emotional need. Could the student have an unmet emotional need that serves as the catalyst for this function? What might it be?

- How would this unmet need contribute to this particular behavior?
- How certain are you that this is the case?
- What evidence do you have that supports this hypothesis?
- What other information do you need to gather?
- Whom might you consult to collect information about your student and their needs?
- What questions do you still have?

Relational need. Could the student have an unmet relational need that serves as the catalyst for this function? What might it be?

- How would this unmet need contribute to this particular behavior?
- How certain are you that this is the case?
- What evidence do you have that supports this hypothesis?
- What other information do you need to gather?
- Whom might you consult to collect information about your student and their needs?
- What questions do you still have?

Control need. Could the student have an unmet control need that serves as the catalyst for this function? What might it be?

- How would this unmet need contribute to this particular behavior?
- How certain are you that this is the case?
- What evidence do you have that supports this hypothesis?
- What other information do you need to gather?
- Whom might you consult to collect information about your student and their needs?
- What questions do you still have?

OK, it's time to make your case for each of the four categories of unmet needs. Imagine you're addressing a panel of professionals who have gathered to discuss your student. Through this process you'll discover which case is the most likely, pressing, or compelling.

Your Turn

Physical Need

Your case: I believe this student's behavior is driven by an unmet physical need because…

_____
_____

Emotional Need

Your case: I believe this student's behavior is driven by an unmet emotional need because…

_____
_____

Relational Need

Your case: I believe this student's behavior is driven by an unmet relational need because…

_____
_____

Control Need

Your case: I believe this student's behavior is driven by an unmet control need because…

_____
_____

Caleb Time

Behavior: Caleb refuses to follow directions much of the day from teachers on any task he doesn't like.

Likely function: Escape/avoidance

Rationale: Caleb shuts down when he is pushed, particularly if the activity includes writing, but anything that requires sustained focus has him refusing or sometimes simply leaving the space.

Case for unmet physical need: I believe Caleb's behavior is driven by an unmet physical need because…

Caleb is often tired and may not be getting enough sleep. He says he sometimes stays up late playing video games, and he is at his worst on these days with very little stamina to try challenging things. There is evidence that Caleb is both overstimulated and understimulated in the classroom. He gets distracted easily, and all the distractions in the room keep his mind from being able to focus. He might benefit from having a smaller space with fewer supplies and materials. Caleb also might need more movement than his peers, which has him getting up and moving throughout the day. It might be beneficial to work in more movement for him—some heavy work where he can stimulate his proprioceptive system. Caleb may also benefit from participating in a sleep challenge between him and me, or maybe Mr. Rios (or maybe the whole class—frankly, many of my students are not getting enough sleep). This is an opportunity to include his family as well in helping him track his hours of sleep. This may serve as an incentive for him to avoid playing video games before bed and to get the benefit of more sleep to help his brain focus better at school.

Case for unmet emotional need: I believe Caleb's behavior is driven by an unmet emotional need because…

When Caleb gets dysregulated, he feels out of control and is not good at calming back down. So when he is calm and regulated, he is reluctant to try anything that may flip his lid. He would benefit from skills to help him calm and regulate himself so he can feel more confident trying hard things. I need to find times and ways to teach him regulation skills, to notice when he is getting upset, and to encourage him to use consistent language to ask for what he needs and practice skills that help him calm down.

Case for unmet relational need: I believe Caleb's behavior is driven by an unmet relational need because…

When Caleb shuts down, he has numerous people come to him to support him and get him back on track. He might be shutting down to connect to and feel seen by others. When he gets up and leaves class, he also has a lot of adults come to him to check in and try to solve the problem. He might benefit from having a champion and having adults set a schedule to regularly check in with him. When he leaves or gets sent out of the classroom, adults should be mindful to not give him too much connection until he has returned to class and made a repair, so they don't accidentally reward him for this behavior. He will need work identifying his needs and practice asking for what he needs.

Case for unmet control need: I believe Caleb's behavior is driven by an unmet control need because…

Caleb has a hard background and needs to feel in control to feel safe. He doesn't fully trust others to take care of him or meet his needs, so he must get his needs met himself. He would likely respond well to choices and compromises (within reason). He may also respond well to having a job or a task to support his struggle with transitions. Because of his struggle with transitions, he needs a consistent schedule and lots of reminders, such as "Caleb, we are getting ready to move away from the reading assignment and prepare for the next subject. Would you please do me a favor and run this envelope across the hallway?" or "Caleb, would you grab the stack of papers on my desk and pass them out to everyone in the class?" or any other sort of job or task that can help him feel a semblance of control while also preparing him for the transition.

Ms. Coombs made a compelling case for each category of need, and her explanations gave Caleb's student support team insights into various possible needs driving his behavior. Because it was not possible to address all areas of need at once, however, the team decided to focus on Caleb's unmet emotional and relational needs as the areas in greatest need of attention.

Your Turn

As you analyze the case you've made for each of the unmet needs, which argument do you find strongest? Which is most likely? Why do you think so?

_____
_____
_____
_____

Which unmet need do you believe is most pressing? Which unmet need, when addressed immediately, might provide your student with the most powerful boost?

_____
_____
_____
_____

Sometimes it is hard to know which unmet need to prioritize first. If you're feeling stuck, and the four cases you presented seem equal in merit and urgency, addressing the following questions can help.

1. Are your tough nugget's basic physical needs being met? Kids don't learn well when they are tired, hungry, thirsty, or sick. If these needs aren't met, this might be a good place to start.

2. Next, look at emotional needs. All children have emotional needs, and many struggle with self-regulation and low attention spans. Many need more frequent breaks, more chances to get the "wiggles" out, and an increased sense of safety. The "way things have always been done" no longer works as well as it used to. It's important to add more regulation supports, reteach social skills and teamwork, and enhance your overall culture and climate. This might be a good place to start if your student's basic physical needs are met.

3. It might benefit some students to prioritize the delivery of extra kindness, reassurance, and other relational needs. If their physical and emotional needs are met, connecting your tough nugget with a consistent, uplifting champion might be the place to start.

4. Finally, you may want to offer the child some more voice and choice in their day, schedule, and routines. This is a good place to start with students who tend to get into power struggles with others.

If you are still unsure, ask a colleague or someone else who knows your student. Remember, you can always ask your student as well. Often their insight is profound and can (and should) lead the way. The key is to open your mind to exploring what your tough nugget needs right now.

Wrapping Up and Looking Ahead

To address the most pressing or impactful unmet need, you (and your team) must now build an intentional intervention plan that meets your student's need in a positive, proactive, consistent way. We'll walk you through that process in Step 7.

STEP 7
Trial and Error (and Trial and Success)

In this chapter, we outline a three-part intervention approach. The first part is the menu. Based on the student need you identified in Step 6 as most pressing, you're going to compile and access a menu of options to meet that need. Why a menu? Because there's no single "right" answer that will work every time, you'll have to select one that you are willing to attempt, that you feel is appropriate for your tough nugget, and that you believe is likely to address the need you've observed. And then you'll go try it out!

The second part is the intervention plan that you'll build for your student. As you construct and employ the plan, consider whether it reinforces actions that are helpful, healthy, and safe for the student's environment. Consider whether (and to what degree) the plan encourages your student to engage in behaviors that are helpful to themselves and to others. Think through how the plan reinforces healthy choices. And remember that your student's safety, and the safety of other students and adults, must remain a priority.

Take your time with this intervention plan. Success doesn't happen overnight. According to the latest research on habit development (Singh et al., 2024), an intervention needs to be implemented consistently for roughly six weeks to be effective. If the intervention is successful in addressing the unmet need (and reducing or eliminating the unhelpful, unhealthy, or unsafe behavior), then you're on to something. If it doesn't work, either revise or refine your application of the strategy, or go back to the menu and try a new strategy. This brings us to the third part of our approach: data collection. We'll keep you focused by providing a place to log your efforts and the results you observe, so you can note the cause-and-effect relationship between the two.

Part A: The Menu

All the strategies offered here belong to one of three buckets we refer to as the "new three *Rs*" in education: relationship, responsibility, and regulation. (Not so coincidentally, these are outlined in detail in Kristin and Pete's [Van Marter Souers with Hall, 2019] book *Relationship, Responsibility, and Regulation: Trauma-Invested Practices for Fostering Resilient Learners*.)

If the unmet need is physical, try one of these strategies from the regulation bucket:

- Talk with the student and their family about setting a regular bedtime and sleep routines.
- Provide additional snacks during the day.
- Encourage the student to eat a full, healthy lunch.
- Take frequent water breaks.
- Consider changing lighting or seating options to allow for movement and change.
- Remove distractors from a space so that the student has fewer things to keep track of.
- Incorporate extra movement throughout the day, including sensory walks and jobs carrying heavy objects, and offer alternative seating on the floor, in a tall chair, or at a standing desk.
- Practice mindfulness or other approaches that allow students to connect with their minds, bodies, and spirits.

Your Turn

What other strategies might you add to this list?

_____

_____

_____

_____

_____

_____

_____

Consult with colleagues and consider other approaches. Why might they work?

_____

_____

_____

_____

_____

_____

_____

If the unmet need is emotional, try one of these strategies, also from the regulation bucket:

- Teach and use brain language (e.g., Dr. Siegel's (2017) "hand model of the brain," mentioned on p. 17).
- Normalize naming and discussing emotions.
- Prioritize three to four self-regulation strategies that work for the student.
- Create a regulation reset space, sometimes referred to as a calming corner, in the classroom that students can access when they notice they are moving to a dysregulated state. Provide options (e.g., therapy putty, colored pencils and paper, fidget toys, a glitter jar) within the space that support students' return to regulation.
- Practice deep-breathing techniques with the student.
- Meet the student at every transition point throughout the day.
- Practice escalating the student through games and simple competition and then regulating with them after.

> **Your Turn**
>
> What other strategies might you add to this list?
>
> _____
>
> _____
>
> _____
>
> _____
>
> Consult with colleagues and consider other approaches. Why might they work?
>
> _____
>
> _____
>
> _____
>
> _____
>
> _____

If the unmet need is relational, try one of these strategies from the relationship bucket (see also the strategies in Chapter 3 [pp. 45–47] and Step 4 [pp. 122–123]):

- Offer compliments, praise, and positive affirmations. Remember the 5:1 ratio: five positive interactions or comments for every correction.
- Ask the student questions about what they're interested in.
- Listen for clues about the student's likes, preferences, goals, and fears.
- Seek out your student during out-of-class time (e.g., library, cafeteria, playground).
- Find ways to make eye contact or appropriate physical touch or to send some type of message throughout the day.

- Invite the student to have a "special spot" in the classroom (to go when they need a reset, or just to feel empowered—you can determine how you do this to set your student up for success).
- Practice repair often.
- Work to make positive interactions with others as quick and predictable as negative interactions can be.

Your Turn

What other strategies might you add to this list?

_____

_____

_____

_____

Consult with colleagues and consider other approaches. Why might they work?

_____

_____

_____

_____

If the unmet need is control, try one of these strategies from the responsibility bucket:

- Offer choice as often as possible (e.g., of partner, topic, pencil, spot in line).

- Teach your student how to compromise: "Come up with a third choice or a choice that meets both your need and my need." (We discuss compromise further in Step 8.)
- Provide options for seating.
- Encourage your student to set learning, behavior, friendship, or other goals.
- Introduce jobs or tasks for students to complete during the day.
- Openly explain the purpose of activities, projects, and learning tasks.
- Help your student build a mental vision of success prior to starting work.
- Provide clear expectations, ask the student to repeat them for clarity, and follow through as the student engages in the tasks.

Your Turn

What other strategies might you add to this list?

_____

_____

_____

_____

Consult with colleagues and consider other approaches. Why might they work?

_____

_____

_____

_____

Part B: The Intervention Plan

It's time to try out a strategy or two for a couple of weeks. Use the form in Figure S7.1 to help you craft your plan (with appreciation to Knoster, 1991, for the elements needed to effect positive change). Remember, you're building a plan to meet your student's need, and you want to find that sweet spot between availability and accountability. Feel free to reference Chapter 6 for suggestions to help you balance your seesaw as you create this plan.

 Your Turn

In Figure S7.1, plug in the strategy (or strategies) you're putting into place, including adequate detail to craft a concrete, deliberate plan to achieve success.

Figure S7.1 Intervention Plan for Your Student

Goal statement: What is the primary unmet need you're attempting to meet/address?

| Strategy
What approach will you take? | Metric
How will you determine whether the intervention is successful? | Skills
What will you and/or the student need for this strategy to take hold? | Motivation
How will you encourage the student to keep trying? How will you keep yourself motivated to stick with it? | Resources
What support (e.g., people, materials, time, space) will you and your student need? | Action Plan
What steps will you take to address the student's unmet need? |
|---|---|---|---|---|---|
| Strategy A: | | | | | |
| Strategy B: | | | | | |

Caleb Time

Caleb's plan: Our team chose to start with two areas that we thought would have the most impact and were doable with our available resources: regulation and relationship skills. To build Caleb's regulation skills, we decided to teach him to ask for what he needs rather than simply doing what he wants. If he could improve in that area, it would help me the most, so we selected that skill to work on first [see Figure S7.2].

Figure S7.2 Intervention Plan for Caleb

Goal statement: What is the primary unmet need you're attempting to meet/address? *Emotional and Relational*

Strategy What approach will you take?	Metric How will you determine whether the intervention is successful?	Skills What will you and/or the student need for this strategy to take hold?	Motivation How will you encourage the student to keep trying? How will you keep yourself motivated to stick with it?	Resources What support (e.g., people, materials, time, space) will you and your student need?	Action Plan What steps will you take to address the student's unmet need?
Strategy A: Teach Caleb the skill of asking for what he needs so he doesn't need to act it out.	Caleb will express his needs and frustration more often and will ask for an intervention that works for him.	• Mindfulness of his emotional state. Caleb will need to be able to identify if he is in his thinking brain or his emotional brain. • Asking for help when stuck Caleb will practice asking for what he needs rather than acting or simply leaving his seat or the class.	To start, the bar will be low and he will be able to get his need met. If Caleb asks appropriately, he will get a "yes" and be allowed to take his break or move seats or take a walk. Once Caleb learns this skill and can ask consistently, we will raise the bar so that he must	• School counselor will teach and practice asking about regulation and check in on Caleb's state daily. • Office will set up a plan so that he can come for his break when he has his special pass, which indicates he asked correctly and got a "yes."	• Teach regulation skills and ask consistently. • Ask Caleb for four ideas of things that he can ask for when he feels overwhelmed. • Report to the team what Caleb is allowed to do when he gets his special pass.

(continued)

Figure S7.2 Intervention Plan for Caleb—*(continued)*

Strategy What approach will you take?	Metric How will you determine whether the intervention is successful?	Skills What will you and/or the student need for this strategy to take hold?	Motivation How will you encourage the student to keep trying? How will you keep yourself motivated to stick with it?	Resources What support (e.g., people, materials, time, space) will you and your student need?	Action Plan What steps will you take to address the student's unmet need?
			complete a certain amount of work before he gets his "yes."		• Collect data on how many times he asks appropriately versus inappropriately.
Strategy B: Meet relational need with all adults, but especially with Ms. C.	Caleb will report that he likes and respects Ms. C. at a 7 or higher and that he feels Ms. C. likes and respects him at a 7 or higher.	N/A	N/A	Ms. C. will be responsible for working on the relationship by connecting with Caleb in multiple ways daily. She needs admin and peers to give her breaks when she needs them so she is more regulated and able to stay calm.	• Ms. C. will ask Caleb the relationship questions and record his answers. • Ms. C. will do a 2x10 with Caleb. • Ms. C. will increase her positive to negative interactions with Caleb to 5:1. • Admin will observe Ms. C. 3 times to track her interactions with Caleb to see her ratio of + to –. • Mr. Rios will check in with Caleb daily to connect and make him feel seen, heard, and valued.

Part C: The Data Collection

For your plan to be successful in the long run, you must implement it with regularity and dedication, collect data consistently, and attend to the direct cause-and-effect relationship between the steps you're taking and the results you're getting. We recommend committing to your plan for four to six weeks to give the intervention time to take hold.

Your Turn

You can use the form in Figure S7.3 to collect data on your efforts and the student outcomes. (*Note:* It might behoove you to consult with your district's behavior specialist or special education administrator, if appropriate, to see if there is a district-supported data collection sheet or process to use. We have heard of times when an educator collected data for weeks, only for the special education department to tell them that the data did not suffice for their needs to determine eligibility toward an IEP, and the educator had to then gather data for another extended period.)

Figure S7.3 Data Collection Form

Student name: _____ Teacher name: _____

Date: _____

Likert scale: 1 = No success, 2 = Limited success,
3 = Mostly successful, 4 = Full success

Time	Context	Intervention attempted	Degree of success (Likert scale)	Anecdotal notes
			1 2 3 4	
			1 2 3 4	
			1 2 3 4	

STEP 7. TRIAL AND ERROR (AND TRIAL AND SUCCESS) 171

Caleb Time

Figure S7.4 shows an example of the data collection form Ms. Coombs filled out during the trial period of Caleb's intervention plan.

Figure S7.4 Data Collection Form for Caleb

Student name: __Caleb__   Teacher name: __Ms. Coombs__
Date: __Dec. 8__

Likert scale: 1 = No success, 2 = Limited success,
3 = Mostly successful, 4 = Full success

Time	Intervention attempted	Degree of success (Likert scale)	Anecdotal notes
Week 1	2x10	1 2 3 **(4)**	I carved out time every day to connect with Caleb and purposefully kept the conversation away from performance. I met my goal this week.
Week 1	5:1 ratio of positive to negative interactions	1 **(2)** 3 4	I haven't done this in a long while and saw how hard it was. The first few days, I struggled to keep up. With some practice, I felt better. At the end, Principal Lewis came in and scored me. During the 20-minute observation, I had a 2.5:1 ratio with Caleb.
Week 1	Giving "yes's"	1 2 **(3)** 4	When Caleb asked to change seats or take a break the right way, I said "yes" and immediately gave him his pass and thanked him for "asking for permission." We keep repeating that phrase so that he associates asking with success and praise. I was successful with this, but his P.E. teacher and one aide struggled to allow him to opt out of work so easily.

(continued)

Figure S7.4 Data Collection Form for Caleb—*(continued)*

Time	Intervention attempted	Degree of success (Likert scale)	Anecdotal notes
Week 1	Practice the skill using a "redo"	1 2 ③ 4	Every time Caleb did something without asking, I did not let him off the hook but made him come back to his seat (or the activity) and ask the right way. As soon as he did so, I said "yes." In this way, I increased the number of practices he got in the day, and he never got rewarded unless he asked correctly.
Week 1	Teaching regulation	1 2 3 ④	The school counselor and I retaught Caleb "flip your lid" and had him make a chart of what he feels when he is in the green, yellow, and red states and brainstormed options of what he can do in each state. (Caleb seems to enjoy the attention he gets as I check in multiple times a day. I tell him what my state is, and he tells me his. It is becoming our special little check-in.)
Week 2	2x10	1 2 ③ 4	This week was clunky; I missed two days with Caleb, and he noticed! He asked about it, which tells me it matters to him. I'll keep going next week.
Week 2	5:1 ratio of positive to negative interactions	1 2 ③ 4	I kept practicing this week. I found it easier to notice and it's becoming more habit. I am finding the language coming easier with other students. My observation with Counselor James had me at a 3.2:1 ratio, so I'm improving!

Time	Intervention attempted	Degree of success (Likert scale)	Anecdotal notes
Week 2	Giving "yes's"	1 2 3 (4)	I continued this week, and it seems to be helping a bit. Caleb is not working much, but he is asking and not simply standing up and disrupting class or walking out. We are spending less time chasing him, which is very helpful!
Week 2	Practice the skill using a "redo"	1 2 3 (4)	The redos really seem to help, and he will come back and do it correctly much more quickly now that he knows it is not a battle, but he simply needs to ask correctly. Next week I will need to start raising the bar and delaying the "yes" a little while I negotiate for some work to be done first.
Week 2	Teaching regulation	1 2 (3) 4	I continue to check in with Caleb often and ask about his regulation state and what he needs to feel calm. We have enlisted an aide to play with him and other boys on the playground, and after they get upset for losing or getting competitive, she has them all stop, tell her their state, and then practice a calming activity. She is really working the four square game, and when Caleb (and others) get out, she has them breathing and using their skills. It seems to be helping Caleb: I watched him walk away and take deep breaths this week. It sure is helping reduce the conflict at four square, too!

Wrapping Up and Looking Ahead

In a perfect world, the intervention plan you've built and implemented works marvelously; your tough nugget's needs are met in a helpful, healthy, and safe manner; their unhelpful, unhealthy, and unsafe behaviors dissipate; and learning and teaching flourish in this newfound state of bliss.

You don't always get a perfect-world outcome, however, so you'll want to be prepared for all possible scenarios. If the plan works, great! You can decide if you want to keep the current interventions in place; slowly reduce the frequency, duration, and intensity of the strategies; or attempt a new intervention to meet another of your tough nugget's needs. If the plan doesn't work, turn to Step 8. We'll walk you through your next steps.

STEP 8

When Things Go Haywire: Response Strategies

OK, so you've tried an intervention plan, and it hasn't yet panned out. You might be feeling frustrated, exhausted, or downright angry about it. Perhaps you just want to scrap everything and begin again. Before you start tossing strategies into the recycling bin, let's back up half a step. How do you know your approaches haven't worked? Look at your data collection form (Figure S7.3, p. 170) and analyze your plan thus far.

Respond to the following questions. We know this undertaking is a lot of work, and because working with other human beings is complex, it will continue to be a heavy lift until you find what's most effective. You may want to share your thoughts with a trusted colleague or bounce ideas off a teammate.

- What is the goal you're trying to achieve with this plan?
- Do you have a clear picture of success in your head? Can you describe it to others?
- To what extent were you (and/or other adults) consistent and intentional about implementing the strategy (be honest)?
- If there were times when you (and/or other adults) weren't consistent or intentional about implementing the strategy, what got in the way?
- To what extent were you (and/or other adults) consistent and intentional about documenting the intervention and the student's resulting behaviors?
- What are some positive results you notice when reviewing the data?
- Do any of the student responses stand out? Why?
- When was the intervention strategy successful? Can you identify a pattern?

- When was the intervention strategy not successful? Can you identify a pattern?
- What does your data review tell you about your goal, your plan, your implementation, and your student's response to it?

Getting to "Just Right": The Five Keys to Effective Discipline

If you're still struggling with your student and their behavior, this is a good time to revisit the keys to effective discipline we introduced in Chapter 6 (see Figure S8.1).

Figure S8.1 The Five Keys to Effective Discipline

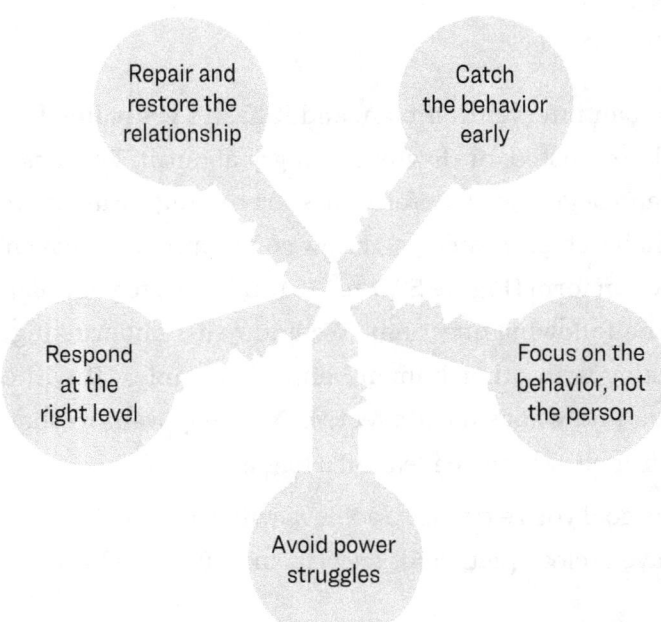

Catch the Behavior Early

If you can notice the behavior and intervene early, then you'll probably need a less intense intervention. When you are attuned to your students—watching their body language, facial expressions, tone of voice, and other outward signals—you'll notice subtle changes that indicate something is affecting their mood or regulation. Good educators know their students well and learn their habits and patterns; great ones notice and catch issues early.

> ### Caleb Time
>
> I have been working hard to check in with Caleb often and notice the signs that he might be escalating. I have been asking him consistently what his "zone of regulation" is so that we are both more aware. I know some of his triggers, like writing, so I have been prompting him and giving him encouragement before and during the activity. As I've gotten to know Caleb better, I've become more attuned to him, which has allowed me to anticipate issues and intervene when a problem is still manageable. I still sometimes do "planned ignoring" for Caleb, but that's when he is being goofy. When Caleb is angry or becoming dysregulated, I cannot ignore it, and intervening quickly has usually helped.

 Your Turn

Are you attuned to your tough nugget and able to see signs of struggle and escalation early?

_____

_____

What do you notice?

_____

_____

When do you see those signs?

_____

_____

How quickly do you take action?
_____
_____

What do you ignore?
_____
_____

What do you address?
_____
_____

Does the student respond differently depending on the timeliness of your intervention? If so, in what ways?
_____
_____

Focus on the Behavior, Not the Person

Addressing the behavior is exactly what it sounds like. The purpose of focusing on the behavior rather than the person is to separate something that *can* be changed, like behavior, from something that *can't*, like personality or temperament.

Another way of looking at this is to focus on what the student is trying to communicate through the behavior. As we discussed earlier, all behavior is communication, and when students have descended into their dysregulated brains, they're less likely to use polite words and socially acceptable actions to communicate their needs to you. Your charge in such a scenario is to unpack the behavior, decipher the message, and focus on what the student is trying to communicate to you rather than how it's being delivered.

In short, if you can focus your perceptions, approaches, thoughts, and comments on the behavior itself instead of the student, then the intervention is more likely to be successful.

Your Turn

Do you find yourself making personality or character statements about your student (even in your own head)?

_____
_____
_____

How do you (or can you) remind yourself to focus on the behavior, not the student?

_____
_____
_____

Caleb Time

Caleb tends to take things personally, so all the adults working with Caleb were asked to talk to him about his actions and behaviors rather than making feedback about his personality. We also all agreed to highlight when he was meeting expectations by saying things like "Caleb, I am really impressed with your focus today." I did this fairly well, and other adults were consistent too, and Caleb responded to this type of address. As time progressed, I realized that I diverged from the plan specifically when I was feeling tired or triggered myself.

Ms. Coombs filled in the chart in Figure S8.2 after we suggested that she try rephrasing some of her comments and even thoughts to focus on the behavior, not on Caleb and his character or personality.

Figure S8.2 Refocusing Comments on the Behavior, Not the Student

Original Teacher Comments/Thoughts	Rephrased Teacher Comments/Thoughts
Caleb is just so lazy.	I wonder what is going on with him that keeps him from engaging.
"Why are you acting like that? What has gotten into you today?"	"What's happening right now that is getting in your way of success?"
"You are being selfish."	"When you don't share with your teammates, it makes it hard for us to work as a team."
Caleb is such a fidget. "Caleb, stop wiggling!"	"Caleb, I notice you are having a hard time sitting still. Do you need a break to help you reset and refocus?"

Avoid Power Struggles

If you've built a suitable nest and you're focused on partnership, connection, and growth, then your intervention is more likely to be successful. Students who struggle with trust or have other underlying unmet needs may dig in and fight, trying to maintain their sense of power and control. This often leads to a power struggle... if you allow it to. Power struggles usually don't end well, because you—the adult, the teacher, the professional—are guaranteed to win, and the student will lose. You didn't enter this profession to force kids to lose, did you?

One way to avoid power struggles is to lower the bar or implement "planned ignoring" (or exasperated ignoring), as Ms. Coombs has done with Caleb. Although that strategy can keep conflict at bay temporarily, it does not change behavior, so you can't use it forever. The goal is to have enough structure to keep the environment safe so that you can teach accountability without igniting constant battles that threaten safety and relationship. With the toughest students, it can be a very difficult line to find, but it is important to continually seek that balance.

Your Turn

How calm are you when dealing with your tough nugget's behavior?

_____

_____

Can you see the need behind that behavior and maintain a high bar while also not getting your buttons pushed?

_____

_____

Do you offer choices and compromises so your student can have some power while you get your needs met too?

_____

_____

Some students need to be taught what a compromise is when they are calm. Does your student need to practice when both of you are calm?

_____

_____

How and when can you do this?

_____

_____

Caleb Time

Caleb is a master of power struggles. He is good at knowing what hooks me in and will play all the strategies to keep me in an argument. Sometimes it seems as if he simply wants to keep me close and is getting an attention need met, but mostly it seems like an avoidance technique because if he can distract and escalate, he often gets out of the assignment or expectation.

To avoid power struggles, I have been practicing the following:

- Stay calm and do not take it personally. I have been doing better at this and not taking his actions so personally, which is really helping with my stress level. I am trying hard to notice that there is a need behind the behavior and to discover what that need might be. The hardest moments for me were when Caleb would look me in the eye and defy my direction, especially in front of all the other students. I would get so angry, but when asked what was behind that anger, I dug deeper and saw that under my anger was fear. Fear that I was failing. Fear that I was losing control. When I realized that my reaction was about me and my own anxieties, I was able to notice and control it a little better.

- Use few words. When responding to his arguments, denials, or questions, I will use no more than 10 words. No lectures or deep explanations, just clear, articulate expectations. I am now fairly good at this skill. I used to talk and explain and go down rabbit holes answering off-topic questions, and that was how Caleb kept me engaged and in an argument. I learned how to shorten my sentences and disengage more quickly and to stop feeling as though I had to respond to everything he had to say. I learned to redirect him to the task at hand. I now say things like "I had no idea that was bothering you. When you finish the current task expectation, we can find a way to address this. For now, let's focus on what the expectation is."

- **Be a broken record.** No matter what Caleb tried to argue or how many questions he asked, I would ignore his comments and repeat the expectation. "I hear you and we can talk about that later. Please sit down and continue writing your story."
- **Offer two fair choices.** Choices help to share power, and they work with Caleb… sometimes. An example of a choice offered is "Would you rather use the standing station, or go sit on the beanbag to finish this task? Which will help you be most successful?"
- **Offer a compromise.** Often Caleb would refuse my two choices, so I did one of two things. First, I allowed for a compromise. This means Caleb is allowed to offer a third choice that gets his need and my need met. Sometimes he would come up with something that I would never have thought of. Once he said he would do his math if he could sit on the floor in the hall. I agreed to this if we could see him, so he sat in the hall in sight of the door, and he was more productive in that quiet environment. Another time he agreed to finally walk back to class if he could swing by the 2nd grade classroom and wave to his sister. This was an easy "yes."

  If there was not enough time for a compromise, or if Caleb was not offering a realistic third option, I would go back to the original two choices and give a time frame, saying, "Caleb, you can do your work at your desk or the table near my desk. You have 20 seconds to decide," and then walking away. Caleb sometimes needs time to process information, and if he is triggered, he automatically wants to argue. My walking away removed the potential for an argument or power struggle while giving Caleb time to consider his options.

Respond at the Right Level

If you respond to your student in a manner consistent with your relationship, appropriate to the intensity of the situation, and in attunement with (your and) your student's emotional state, then the intervention is more likely to be successful.

Responding appropriately to a student's challenging behavior is a complex endeavor. Rarely, if ever, is there a positive and productive *If student does* X, *you respond with* Y equation. If anyone ever tells you they have The Answer, take that claim with a very large grain of salt. The most honest approach to student behaviors, classroom management, and discipline is "It depends."

Your response depends on two key things. First, what is the strength of your relationship with the student? We've focused quite a bit on relationships in this workbook, because we know that there are times when you'll need to leverage that relationship to push and demand more from your students. These interactions will be much more positive and productive if they're coming from a strong foundation of connection, trust, respect, and genuine caring. Second, what is the *state* you and your student are in? By *state,* we're referring to the degree to which you're both regulated. You, as the adult, need to be calm and regulated, and you should respond according to the level of your student's regulation state.

The following "Levels of Response" come from the "correcting principles" of Trust-Based Relational Intervention (TBRI), which is an attachment-based, trauma-informed intervention that is designed to meet the complex needs of vulnerable children (Purvis et al., 2013). These levels "identify responsive practices that are matched in intensity to the level of risk or challenge, and yet are purposeful in maintaining the connection with the child or youth" (Purvis et al., 2013, para. 42). Although the TBRI model includes four levels of response, here we provide guidance only on the first three because the fourth level addresses a "significant threat of violence or harm by the child," and we advise school personnel to pursue specialized training that meets your local legal and regulatory requirements.

Level One: Playful Engagement

Playful engagement means that you handle the misbehavior with a light tone and the goal of avoiding a power struggle. If you look your toughest, most oppositional students in the eye and firmly say, "Stop that" or even "Please stop that," they might ignore you or even look you back in the eye and say in some form or another, "Make me." The goal of a Level One response is to avoid that.

To be clear, we are not talking about being "soft" here. To be successful, you must maintain your high standards. You are not lowering the bar. You are clear and firm in your expectations, and your language, tone, and body are all relaxed and nonconfrontational. All these factors help to keep you out of power struggles. Remember, students from hard places are on a constant lookout for danger in their environments. They misinterpret positive responses as neutral, neutral responses as negative, and negative responses as threatening. Therefore, you are careful to not trigger their sensitive stress response systems with signs of threat.

Caleb Time

For Caleb, we found that no one was doing playful engagement. Most of his initial prompts from me were for very small things. Caleb tires me out, so I was trying to notice and intervene at even the slightest hint at escalation, but that meant I was always on his back and giving him negative attention.

I honestly didn't know what to do differently, so I had to ask for some help and coaching and was asked to try being playful and light at the beginning. I practiced some phrases and worked on saying them with a smile on my face and in my voice, even if I didn't feel it inside. I tried things like "Caleb, you've sure got the wiggles today. Why don't you wiggle your way back to your desk? It's time to get started." and "Caleb, you have your wandering legs on again. Please put your sitting legs on for a few more minutes, and then we will have a chance to move." I also used the phrase "Let's try that again" anytime he was out of line, and as our relationship and trust grew, he began to do his redo more quickly and easily, and we were able to move on.

As I practiced these phrases, I noticed a small change in Caleb, but a bigger change in myself. I was less uptight and lighter in general, and I think that helped the whole class.

> **Your Turn**
>
> At Level One, how does the student respond to playful engagement?
> _____
> _____
> _____
>
> Do you have a handful of phrases that might help you connect with your student?
> _____
> _____
> _____
>
> Would starting with lightness and a reminder of the expectation help your student feel less in trouble (and therefore less likely to be triggered)?
> _____
> _____
> _____

Level Two: Structured Engagement

Sometimes playful engagement doesn't work, and your students need a stricter, more structured intervention to get back on track. The following are some ways you can provide that structure.

Use physical proximity. Move close to the student so you can use a low voice. Disciplining from across the room can be embarrassing and requires a louder voice, both of which can be triggering for a student. So get close and get their attention.

> ### Caleb Time
> When playful engagement does not work and Caleb refuses to comply, I am working my Level Two skills by calmly walking toward him, lowering my voice, and setting the expectation for him to return to his seat. When I don't direct him from across the room, thus avoiding having all the students witness the redirection, Caleb usually doesn't escalate so quickly and is less defensive.

Speak in a soft voice. The words themselves don't matter nearly as much as the tone, volume, and intensity they're spoken in. It's important to practice not only kind words but also a kind voice. By using a technique called "whisper discipline" or the "whisper method," the adult can shift from a "teacher voice" to a "whisper voice," which means slower, lower, and quieter. The goal is to help keep the student calm so they can work with you through the problem.

Offer acceptable choices. Offering choices is helpful, and most educators are well versed in this strategy. However, in the moment, when a student's behavior is overwhelming and affecting others, our options aren't always easy to identify. We give choices to share power and help the student stay in their prefrontal cortex, so they can think about the problem without having their limbic system take over. Thinking through choices in advance can be very helpful, because you'll want to offer the student two reasonable options that you can live with. What you *don't* want to do is offer choices that clearly have a right or wrong answer, like "Would you rather do your work at your desk or in the principal's office after school?" That's called an ultimatum, and it's a one-way ticket to a power struggle.

Here are some examples of acceptable choices:

- "Would you like to walk back to class by yourself or with Mr. Johnson?"
- "Would you like to join the group on the carpet or in the chair on the side?"
- "Would you like to work at your desk or use the standing station?"

Notice that the expectation of each of these choices is clear, and remember: The goal of a choice is to share power. If the student refuses, starts to argue, or is stuck in their dysregulated brain and cannot answer, try one of the following two structured engagement strategies.

Add a time frame. Some students need a bit of time to consider the choices and what they want. They might have slow verbal processing skills and need a moment. Other students find your presence to be triggering (either it's too intense or it propels their desire to be oppositional). Either way, it can be helpful to offer a choice with a time frame and then disengage for a moment. Here's an example: "I am going to give you 30 seconds to make a helpful and healthy choice. I have full faith in your ability to get back to your seat."

Invite a compromise. Even though you may be averse to the thought of compromising with a student who has broken a rule and done something that's not OK, a compromise can help you avoid a standoff. When a student says "no" or otherwise refuses to choose, rather than saying, "Either you choose or I'll choose for you," try saying this to get unstuck: "It sounds like you're asking for a compromise." This statement sends the signal that there is even more power to be shared, can get some students moving who are completely frozen in the moment, and teaches a valuable life lesson: how to negotiate your needs.

Will this approach work? It depends. More often than not, yes. That said, some students can't handle choices, let alone propose a compromise. In such a case, or in the case of students who propose outlandish ideas, prefer to argue, or refuse to negotiate, you simply need to give clear, calm directives.

Caleb Time

When none of the other methods worked, I tried working through a compromise with Caleb. I would say, "Wow, today is one of those rough days. It sounds like we need to come up with a compromise. What do you need to be able to get back to work? What is a choice you can make that will support your learning and not disrupt my teaching and the learning of your teammates?" Caleb and I would work together to identify possible alternatives to get him back on track. One of the options he would ask for was to work with a buddy. We would identify expectations for what that could sound like and look like. I would share the expectations of what I expected to see. In general, though certainly not always, Caleb responded better when he was not pushed and had a voice in the matter.

Your Turn

At Level Two, how often do you give direction and correction from across the room?
___
___

Would it be helpful for your tough nugget if you moved closer and used a quieter, more private voice?
___
___

When you offer choices, how does your student respond?
___
___

Check your choices: Do you tend to offer two fair choices, or an ultimatum?
___
___

How is your student's response different depending on the nature of the choices?
___
___

When you include a time frame or walk away to give space, how does your student respond?
___
___

> Is your student able to compromise? How does that play out?
>
> _____
>
> _____
>
> How might you remind yourself to access these Level Two strategies on a regular basis?
>
> _____
>
> _____

Level Three: Calming Engagement

If your attempts at Levels One and Two are not resulting in the desired outcome, your student might just need a break from the setting—and frankly, you may need a break from the student. If either of you begins to respond out of emotion and a lid flip is imminent (or occurs), those prefrontal cortex skills (e.g., empathy, long-term planning, cause and effect, language) become inaccessible, and continuing the conversation will likely lead to further escalation. Although it isn't the ideal solution, there are times when you will need to initiate an exit. If it comes to this point, the following strategies may help.

Be attuned to signs of dysregulation. Look for signals from the student—and yourself—that the emotional response has reached a breaking point. If either you or the student becomes dysregulated, it is the adult's responsibility to notice, de-escalate, or disengage. Take a break and table the conversation until cooler heads can prevail.

Speak succinctly. When it comes to hard conversations, discipline, and high emotion, it is best to keep sentences short and language clear. Use as few words as possible to convey your message. Here are some examples:

- "I can see you are upset. Go ahead and take a seat over there, and we can talk when you feel calmer."
- "When you talk to me with that tone, that tells me you are getting angry. Please take a moment here, and I'll come back in a few minutes when you feel more regulated."

- "I'm getting frustrated, so I need a moment. I will come back and discuss this with you when I have taken a few breaths and calmed down."
- "You are getting really riled up. Come here and sit near me, and when you have regulated a little bit, you can join your group again."

Caleb Time

Caleb flips his lid fairly easily, so it can be hard to solve problems with him. I can see that when I engage with him while he is upset, things tend to get worse. It is hard for me to leave him alone in those moments because I am afraid I might not get him back, but I am practicing walking away and giving us both a break. I found that setting a timer helps us both; he knows I'll be back in a few minutes, and I won't forget him and let him sit in the hall for too long (which has happened a couple of times in the past).

I have been working with our classroom aide and having her also practice using very few words and not engaging in arguments or power struggles. This is also helping. As she engages less, Caleb tends to escalate less.

Your Turn

At Level Three, how can you remind yourself to remain vigilant to signs of dysregulation (in your student and yourself)?

_____

_____

What are some words and phrases you could prepare in advance, should you need to pause the conversation and take a break?

_____

_____

> What are some healthy, safe options for how and where your student can de-escalate and self-regulate? When can you practice this?
>
> _____
>
> _____

Repair and Restore the Relationship

Exiting an interaction with a student isn't always easy, nor is it pleasant. Often, even though it's warranted, taking a break can result in hard feelings and a rupture to the relationship. The key is that you are willing to repair with your student when it does happen. It's important to remember that the relationship is more important than the offense, and if you commit to repairing the relationship whenever it's needed, then the intervention is more likely to be successful.

In *Fostering Resilient Learners,* Kristin and Pete (Souers with Hall, 2016) outlined six steps for effective communication: listen, reassure, validate, respond, repair, and resolve. Repair is one of the steps that often gets skipped, but one of the most crucial:

> A repair includes a heartfelt apology for whatever role you may have played in the miscommunication or strife. Even if you don't believe you were in the wrong, an earnest apology can go a long way in building trust. It doesn't necessarily mean you're accepting responsibility for what took place, just that you can recognize the other person's experience and are sorry things turned out the way they did. And when you *do* have some responsibility for the situation, acknowledging your part in it honestly and humbly can lead to great strides in building trust and relationship. The goal of repair is to attempt to heal the rupture in the relationship and to begin identifying alternative ways of managing to avoid a similar disruption in the future. (Souers with Hall, 2016, p. 77)

Your Turn

Do you have a system for giving a time and place for a repair conversation?
___
___

Have you taught your students (and adult colleagues, too!) the tools for making an effective repair?
___
___

How often do you repair with your tough nugget?
___
___

Do you come back to your student, who may be mad at you for holding them accountable (or whom you have expressed frustration toward), and have a conversation and work on the repair with them?
___
___

Have you been too permissive with your tough nugget? Too regimented?
___
___

How are you balancing availability with accountability?
___
___

Caleb Time

When Caleb would leave the classroom, or when he was sent out—either way—there was always a talented, kind, and well-meaning adult who supported him and brought him back, usually feeling calmer and ready to learn. Caleb and I sometimes had a short conversation, but often we just moved on as if nothing had happened. Over time, my frustration and resentment grew because nothing ever seemed to be resolved.

Our team put in place one intervention, which was to say that Caleb would not be sent back to class until he was ready to repair with me or the classroom aide, whomever he had the conflict with. The staff member, after helping Caleb regulate and agree to a repair, would call the classroom and ask if I was ready for him to repair and then return to class. When I was ready, the assistant principal would cover the class while Caleb and I talked in the hallway. Here's how a repair conversation might go:

Me: "Caleb, that was a bit of a mess, wasn't it? I am really glad we are having this conversation so we can work toward making things better."

Caleb: "Yes. I'm glad we are talking, too."

Me, demonstrating respect and taking responsibility: "Caleb, I hope you know that you are important to me, and I want you in my class. I am sorry for getting frustrated with you. I know that wasn't helpful. It is hard having to send you out of class, and I'm sorry we weren't able to work that out in the classroom. It would have been really nice for you to stay and keep learning."

Caleb: "I'm sorry I didn't follow directions."

Me, accepting the apology and reiterating the expectations: "I appreciate that, Caleb. And it's not just that you didn't follow directions, because we can almost always work out a deal together. It surprised me that today we didn't find that compromise. Did I do something that upset you? If so, I'm sorry; I *didn't realize it. I want us to work together, and I want to help you when things start to become hard."*

Caleb: *"No, I've just been having a bad day, I guess."*

Me: *"This is a great example of something we can work on together. If you are having a hard day, I want you to tell me right away. That way, we can come up with some ideas to help you stay focused and learn even when things are hard. Do you want to talk about why you are having such a bad day? You know, you can talk to me about anything."*

Caleb: *"No, I just had a moment."*

Me: *"I see. In the future, let me know if you're having a moment sooner, so we can choose to self-regulate in the classroom without having to go to the office. I can help with that, you know. Just show me the hand signal."*

Caleb, showing the hand signal: *"You mean this one?"*

Me: *"That's the one. Are you ready to go back inside and get to learning?"*

Caleb, smiling: *"Yes."*

Your Turn

Jot down some ideas of what you can say when repairing with your tough nugget. What are some of the key messages you want to convey to your student when engaging in this essential step?

_____

_____

_____

_____

Wrapping Up and Looking Ahead

There may come a time when your efforts aren't yielding the results you're aiming for. In fact, you may arrive at a place where you're throwing up your hands and are desperate for help. Because of the intensity, frequency, or duration of the incidents, you may become completely overwhelmed and in need of outside support.

And that's OK. Offer yourself some grace and be OK with the fact that you're human—your strategies and approaches aren't perfect. Let's face it: *Nobody* is perfect. Working with children is complex, and sometimes you need different eyes and a different angle to address your issues. The reality is that many students are struggling right now and lack the skills to regulate effectively. Some truly do need additional support. Just as you encourage your students to ask for help when needed, you need to be able to do the same.

Help is here, in the form of your colleagues and your team, which we'll explain in Step 9. Sometimes you need to send up the bat signal.

STEP 9

The Bat Signal: Calling on Outside Support

Help is here—usually in the form of colleagues, teammates, and other adults. If you work at a typical school, you'll have a built-in team, and we suggest that you expand the team to include other adults who "share the care" for your student, such as parents or caregivers, after-school program staff, support staff, custodians, cafeteria workers, bus drivers, sports coaches, and so on; be creative and reflect on who has a relationship with your tough nugget.

The first step is to send up a flare, or what we call the bat signal. You probably recognize when an issue is too big for you to solve on your own or when your student presents with more severe concerns that require more intensive and comprehensive resources, supports, and plans for intervention. Schools will always have a handful of students who need this level of intervention. The key for you is to have strong universal practices in place (described throughout Part 1) and to have intentionally attempted individualized interventions for the student who needs just a bit more (described in Steps 1–8 in Part 2).

Ideally, your setting has a protocol in place to allow this to happen. It might be called a child study team, a student success team, an MTSS team, or a site-specific acronym. Ask around if you don't know what the process is for getting help! A setting with such a protocol would have an allotted time for staff to come together and support students who have greater needs. If you *don't* have a protocol or allotted time for this work in your existing practice, then we advise that you consider these recommendations and add them if possible.

Identify Who Needs to Be on the Team

The people invited to the table form the team, so it's important to be clear and intentional about those invitations. Here are some questions to help you form the team and set the stage for its members to be successful in supporting you and your tough nugget:

- Who needs to be invited to the meeting to support your student? Consider the value added by including your tough nugget's parent or guardians, former teachers, classified staff, specialists, counselors, and others who interact with the child.
- How do you communicate with them? How do you share the urgency of your request?

Run an Intentional Meeting

Once the date, time, and location of the meeting are established, work with whichever key personnel at your site manages these meetings to build an agenda. When you meet as a team, here are some questions to consider:

- What community agreements will you set for staying strength focused, goal oriented, on task, and supportive?
- What steps will you go through?
- What information is pertinent?
- How will you share the observations, reflections, data, and other information you've gathered through the course of this workbook? That information is gold, and including it is essential in this "teaming" step!

There are many ways to run a successful problem-solving meeting (and a few ways to run a bad one). We have used the following approach to keep the meeting focused and productive.

First, we ask the staff member who is bringing a student to the attention of the team to prepare by responding to the following questions before the meeting:

- What are the strengths of the student? (This helps get us started on the right foot.)
- What are the one or two most pressing challenges? (This helps prioritize and focus the educator.)
- What do you think the need behind the behavior is? (This helps the educator start thinking beyond surface behaviors.)

- Which interventions have you tried, and what have the results been? (A brief history of interventions already attempted ensures that the team won't spend time suggesting ideas that have already been tried.)
- What does the student say the issue is? Have they offered possible solutions? (Asking the student is an essential step in the process.)

The answers to these questions provide focus and vital background so that the meeting can be efficient and productive.

Once in the room, the team members, who have already read the answers to the preceding questions, can get right to business. The following protocol was developed for a 15-minute meeting but can be adapted for 12 minutes or expanded for longer sessions.

1. The presenting educator provides an overview of the student, including strengths, issues, and an essential question for the group. (Four minutes)
   - No matter how long this section is, it is important to time it. Keeping this first part short requires the educator to be concise and ensures the meeting doesn't get bogged down with a long explanation that simply admires the problem.
2. The team asks clarifying questions. (Three minutes)
   - Again, this part is short. It is important for team members to ask questions and not offer solutions yet.
3. The team discusses and offers possible interventions and solutions. (Four minutes)
   - During this step, while the team members speak openly, it is key that the presenter does not speak. Have you ever been in a problem-solving session where every solution offered was met with a "Yeah, but…" or a "That won't work because…"? Immediate responses to ideas often take all the air out of the room, leaving everyone feeling stuck.
4. The presenter shares which ideas were helpful or what they would like to try. (Two minutes)
   - The presenter can now discuss what they thought was helpful. They can simply ignore and let go of any ideas that they have tried before or don't think will work.
5. The facilitator wraps up and summarizes next steps. (Two minutes)

- The facilitator concludes the meeting, summarizing what was agreed on, assigning tasks as needed, and setting any follow-up dates.

Whether or not you use this protocol, the following are key to a successful problem-solving meeting:

- Have a facilitator who is willing to organize and time each segment.
- Ensure the description of the problem is brief so there is enough time to get to solutions.
- Allow a brainstorming session that is free from denials or rebuttals from the presenter.
- Give the presenter permission to disregard suggestions that don't feel right and focus on ideas that seem helpful and possible.

Create a Plan

If you leave the meeting with a concrete plan with all the essential components (goals, both short-term and long-term; specific steps; timeline; person responsible for each step; resources needed; accountability partners; evidence of success; and so on), you'll be in good shape. If your team has a process and template already, that's great! Use them. If not, feel free to go back to the one we offer in Step 7 (Figure S7.1, p. 166), and update it as needed.

Follow Through

If you have a plan, everyone must stick to it. There must be mutual accountability structures built in, so you can help (and nudge) one another through the process. This includes (1) setting up formal follow-up meetings in advance and (2) establishing a protocol for teammates to request help and ideas from one another when the going gets tough between meetings. This is probably the period when we most frequently see interventions fall apart. Following through with consistency and regularity, especially when the results aren't immediately evident and overwhelmingly successful, can be a challenge. Here are some questions and prompts that can help:

- Review the plan that you've created as a team.
- What, exactly, does it require you to do?
- How might you maintain the solution-oriented, optimistic headspace and heartspace needed to incorporate the strategies in the spirit they were intended?

- If you're struggling with this, who can help?
- If your teammates are struggling with this, how can you help?
- Identify times when the strategies are effective. What conditions support that success?
- When the strategies aren't effective, why not? What's different?
- How might you replicate the situations in which the interventions have been successful?
- How can you maintain the energy and momentum you need to keep trying?
- What support do you need to keep supporting your student?

Caleb Time

It's been a couple of months since I started this process and went through all the steps. Things are still not perfect, and Caleb continues to have some bad days, but they do not affect me so strongly. First, it seems like the bad days are the exception now, so they don't scare me as much. Before, when I was completely stuck, I felt hopeless and unsure how I would make it through a whole year like this. Now, though it is still hard at times, it doesn't feel so overwhelming and there is hope. For one thing, Caleb has better and safer relationships with many adults. I asked him again the other day whether he likes me and if he thinks I like him. His answer this time was quick! He said yes and gave a score of 9/10 to both questions. I asked what I could do to make it a 10/10 and he was not sure. This is a good sign, though, and I know I am enjoying him a lot more now as well.

We are now able to use the power of our relationships with Caleb to negotiate discipline, and he will let us! Before, it seemed that he didn't care how his behavior and attitude affected anyone else. This, all on its own, has been a big relief. A huge change with this is our training for staff on how to avoid power struggles. We are no longer rewarding him with our attention when he argues and have been consistent in making him come back and do it right (like ask with respect or ask for what he needs). This has saved us all a lot of angst and time, too.

I really believe that I can see Caleb's brain rewiring! By consistently working on safety and clear expectations, Caleb is learning to be a part of the system, and it is so cool to see. His awareness of his own regulation is getting better, and he will share how he feels with me, so I can help him work through it, and he has gotten much better at simply asking for what he needs. He has learned the skill of asking for a break, so he no longer just walks off. He also rarely simply ignores adults and continues to do what he wants. He will stop and talk with an adult, and we can work through it. The other day, I told Caleb that a secretary was having a really hard day and could use a smile. Caleb walked down the hall, greeting the people he passed, and smiled at the secretary. This was the happiest I've seen him and one of the first real displays of empathy I have seen from him. How exciting!

The whole class seems to be doing better, too. I attribute this partly to Caleb being less unpredictable and disruptive, but also to my own work staying calm and practicing being light in my tone and demeanor, even when things are stressful. The mood of the class has shifted, and that feels great.

Caleb still balks at writing and math much of the time and is still behind academically. We will just need to keep working at it, though he is in class more and is more productive at this time, so we are heading in the right direction. Caleb also is a sore loser and doesn't do well when he feels like he is failing. We have work to do to teach him how to lose with grace and not be afraid of mistakes.

We know that home can be stressful at times, that his sleep is irregular, and that sometimes he is allowed to play video games or watch scary and violent movies late into the night. This is mostly out of our control, and since we don't

> have a social worker, it is hard to find the time to engage the whole family. We know that Caleb would be better if we could somehow get his family on board and increase their skills at discipline and enforcing family rules (it appears that Caleb wears them down with his arguing and sometimes wins when he escalates, so parents are stuck). I've told this to my admin and counselor and will leave it to them to continue to support this family. In the meantime, I'll keep focusing on what I have control over and continue to give Caleb the safe, kind, and predictable repetitions that are helping him grow.

Wrapping Up and Looking Ahead: Celebrate and Calibrate

Calling in reinforcements does not mean you're a bad educator or you've lost the battle. It could simply mean the challenge is formidable. It could require some skills that you don't have. It could necessitate a shift in some schoolwide procedures that you can't control. It could indicate that the intervention needs more time to take hold. There are a million reasons why you might need to send up a bat signal and ask for help, but the most convincing, powerful, and compelling one is that your student, your child, your tough nugget needs it!

In the meantime, don't lose sight of the fact that things *will* go well. Not everything, but some things. Please make it a priority to celebrate the little successes along the way. Celebration is contagious. Along the same lines, when things *don't* go well, rather than get discouraged and frustrated, refocus your energy on your goal, the mindsets you need to bring to the table, and the possibility of success down the road. Remaining grounded, and keeping your team grounded, can help in times of turbulence and difficulty.

Conclusion to Part 2

Over the course of your career, you'll encounter students for whom the first intervention works perfectly, and you'll find yourself looking in the mirror thinking, "You're brilliant!" Other times, your attempts may fall flat or even exacerbate the issues in front of you. Be careful not to succumb to negative self-talk, because here's the reality: This work is hard, and rarely will you find a strategy that works universally. Of course you're brilliant, *and* you'll need to keep going back to the drawing board, to the well, to the supply closet, to the resource shelves to find new and different approaches to meet your students' varying needs.

Often, when things are going poorly, the first inclination is to switch strategies. This is necessary sometimes. But before you do, consider this question: "How many repetitions does it take to learn a complex skill?" Let's say you want to learn to play the guitar. How many repetitions does it take before you can move between three chords without looking at your fingers? Quite a few, right? If a skill is very complex, it could take thousands of repetitions before it becomes second nature. So if you are giving a student consistent, repetitive practice with a complex skill like regulation and you are not seeing much success, please don't lose hope. Even if you are doing everything just right, the results might be hundreds of repetitions down the road. And even as you are doing your part, there are times when you'll need to wave your arms and request support, because some students need more repetitions and interventions than you are able to give. Next year's teacher will thank you for your diligence and fortitude, as will your student's family and the larger community. By staying in the game and continuing to do your best every day, you are ensuring your efforts will pay off in the long run.

Because there are so many children who need additional help and support, it's a good thing we have people like you in the profession. You're "in it to win it," as they say.

You're dedicated to finding ways to encourage the healthy growth and development of your students. For that, we'll finish with the same two words that launched this workbook: Thank you.

Acknowledgments

This workbook is a continuation of our quest to shift the conversations about children, education, and trauma to a more productive, solution-oriented, collaborative approach. We realize it is but a tool, one that must be in the hands of educators and caregivers to fulfill its purpose of influencing their heads and hearts. In that light, we're eternally grateful to Genny Ostertag, our incomparably extraordinary editor Miriam Calderone, and the rest of the magnificent team at ASCD who had the forethought and commitment to publish our first book, *Fostering Resilient Learners,* in 2016—before "trauma" became a mainstream topic. In this world, we can either lead or follow, and we're grateful for having the opportunity to serve as part of the leadership of this discussion and this important work.

No workbook, textbook, guidebook, or any other book would be worth anything without readers, and if not for the hundreds of thousands of readers of *Fostering Resilient Learners* and its follow-up companion, *Relationship, Responsibility, and Regulation,* we wouldn't be here with number three. The reaction we've gotten to the first two books has been both heartwarming and heart-wrenching, filling us with pride in their impact and a yearning to do more. This workbook truly is a response to the feedback, requests, and cries from our readers for exactly that: more. It is our sincere and earnest hope that this supports all of you in your endeavor to do right by your children, your students, your communities, and yourselves.

Finally, special thanks to all the "Calebs" out there who have confused and confounded us and taught us valuable lessons about how to be grounded and successful in tough situations.

APPENDIX

Prompts and Templates

Appendix: Prompts and Templates

Welcome to the Appendix. You're here because you've successfully completed the process of analyzing and addressing your tough nugget's needs, and you've likely realized that you have another student, or more, who could benefit from this process. Rather than send you back to the bookstore, or even back through the entire text of this workbook, we've provided a streamlined compilation of the templates and prompts from the Your Turn sections from Part 2 that you can use as your guide on the side as you consider your next "Caleb." This packet is also available to download as a PDF from http://www.ascd.org/fostering-resilience-elementary-forms and www.fosteringresilientlearners.org/other-resources. Feel free to consider each question and situation thoroughly, and take your time—it's better to do this work well than to do it fast. Of course, if you want to retrace some of your steps and reread the sections of the workbook that accompany these prompts, feel free. This resource is here for you to use as you need it. Thank you for your commitment to your students.

Step 1. Who's the Child?

Student name: _____

Grade: _____

List your student's strengths, positive attributes, and resiliency factors. Consider questions such as the following to prompt your summary of what makes your student awesome:

What does this student like?

_____

_____

Who are they connected to?

_____

_____

What are things they are doing well?

_____

_____

Where are they succeeding?

_____

_____

What makes them smile and feel happy?

_____

_____

What are they good at?

_____

_____

What do they want to be when they grow up?

_____

_____

When they are at their best, what is fun and likable about them?

_____

_____

What would their family member (or someone who loves them a lot) say is great about them?

_____

_____

What are some strengths you've noted about your student's family?

_____

_____

What is your goal for this student?

_____

_____

Have you talked with other adults in the school about your student and how they perform outside your classroom? What have you discovered? How universal are the issues?

_____

_____

_____

Have you talked with past teachers or schools? What have you found out? Is this a new issue or one that has been around for a while?

_____

_____

_____

Have you spoken with other caregivers and family members about your student? Are they experiencing similar struggles, or do they have different experiences?

_____

_____

_____

What has been effective in the past?

_____

_____

_____

What insights or advice might they offer?

_____
_____
_____

Is there a past 504/IEP/behavior intervention plan on file? If so, what's included in it?

_____
_____
_____

Can you stitch together a family history? What are your student's family situation and dynamics, child welfare history, school performance, diagnosis (if any), and past resources and needs?

_____
_____
_____

Step 2. Complicating Factors and "How You Doin'?"

What's getting in the way of your student's success? (Be specific.)

___

What happens to you when you think of this student?

___

What do you think?

___

How do you feel?

___

What happens in your body—do you feel any anxiety, worry, sadness, or fear? If so, how does it manifest?

_____

_____

_____

What story are you telling yourself about this student or the situation?

_____

_____

_____

What are you afraid of?

_____

_____

_____

What do you need at this time to focus on the needs of the student?

_____

_____

_____

Step 3. Culture of Safety

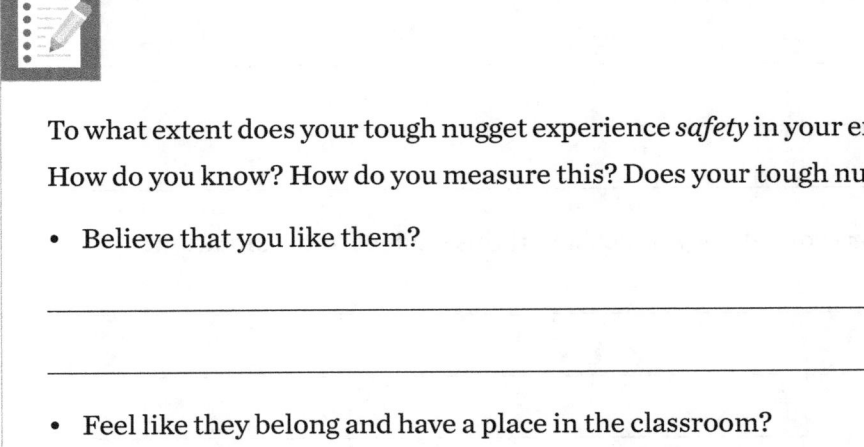

To what extent does your tough nugget experience *safety* in your environment? How do you know? How do you measure this? Does your tough nugget...

- Believe that you like them?

_____

_____

- Feel like they belong and have a place in the classroom?

_____

_____

- Believe they can be vulnerable and make mistakes?

_____

_____

- Have opportunities to understand and uncover their emotions?

_____

_____

- Have the opportunity to be themselves without being teased or bullied?

_____

_____

- Believe they are capable of being successful in your environment?

_____

_____

To what extent does your environment support regulation and safety?

- Does your tough nugget have sensory issues that get in their way of being comfortable or safe?

  _____

  _____

- Does the lighting need to be changed or do seating choices need to be offered to meet some basic physical or physiological needs?

  _____

  _____

To what extent does your tough nugget experience *predictability* in your environment? How do you know? How do you measure this?

- What visual reminders do you have of your norms, expectations, and schedule?

  _____

  _____

- Are routines and schedules established?

  _____

  _____

- When there are changes to a routine or schedule, are there prompts and reminders so students can prepare?

  _____

  _____

To what extent does your tough nugget experience *consistency* in your environment? How do you know? How do you measure this?

- Are you calm and grounded each day, so students experience you in a similar way despite your own stress level or workload?

  _____

  _____

- Do all staff members respond in consistent ways to positive as well as disruptive behaviors?

  _____

  _____

- Is there a common language for teaching and responding to misbehavior in different environments throughout the school?

  _____

  _____

Are there changes you can put in place that will help increase safety and regulation for your student, such as reconsidering their seating location? Increasing seating options? Reducing overstimulation by changing lights or minimizing clutter? Reducing understimulation by allowing for breaks and movement throughout the day? What skills are missing for your student that you can teach proactively when both you and they are calm? You might want to access your student's responses to the Safety Survey (see Figure 2.1 on p. 37) to inform your decision making.

Step 4. Fostering Connections

What is your relationship with this student?
_____
_____
_____

When were you last in sync? Is there something specific to which you can attribute that rapport?
_____
_____
_____

When did you last experience a rift? What, specifically, caused it?
_____
_____
_____

On a scale of 1–10, how much do you like and respect this student? (*Note:* If your number is 7 or below, revisit Step 1. If that doesn't help you see your student in a warmer, more human way, poll some colleagues and find some things to like and appreciate about your kiddo.)
_____
_____
_____

On a scale of 1–10, how much would this student say you like and respect them? (*Note:* Even if you are working to find things to like about your student, if they don't feel it or believe it, you will need to do more work here. Some students take a long time to get through to, so keep sending the message that you are on their side.)

_____

_____

_____

On a scale of 1–10, how much does this student like and respect you? (*Note:* This is another indicator of relationship, and if the score is 7 or below, you will need to start here.)

_____

_____

_____

Relationship *has* to be at the forefront. If any of these questions gets a score of 7 or below, you must stop working on problem solving, goal setting, and behavior change and refocus on relationship building and safety.

Which of the six connection strategies (see pp. 122–123) are you willing to employ?

_____

_____

_____

Why do you think it will be successful?

_____

_____

_____

What is your ratio of positive to negative interactions with your tough nugget?

_____

_____

_____

Commit to using one of the strategies for two weeks. Much like a 2x10, if you apply it with consistent effort, you're likely to see results. Keep some anecdotal notes on your progress in the "Notes on Strategy Progress" form on the next page.

Notes on Strategy Progress

Strategy selected: _____

Date	Notes on Student's Response to the Strategy

How does your tough nugget like to be praised?

_____
_____
_____

Are you noticing when your student is doing well, even when the positive behavior is small or expected?

_____
_____
_____

Does your student have a champion?

_____
_____
_____

With whom does your student tend to interact positively?

_____
_____
_____

How could you determine which adults are in a position of trust and connection with your student?

_____
_____
_____

What steps could you take to find a suitable champion for your student?

_____
_____
_____

What does your student have to say about the adults in their orbit?

_____
_____
_____
_____

To what extent does your student connect with peers?

_____
_____
_____

Does your tough nugget work well with others?

_____
_____
_____

Who are your student's friends?

_____
_____
_____

When other students talk with your tough nugget, do they use their name?

_____
_____
_____

To what extent is your student included in activities, group projects, stories, jokes, special events, and other opportunities for peers to gather?

_____
_____
_____

What windows are open for you to enlist the efforts of peers to include your tough nugget?

_____
_____
_____

What opportunities do you have to partner your tough nugget with a younger student to be a mentor, or an older student to have a "big buddy" of some kind?

_____
_____
_____

How might your student offer a service to the school or community using their skills, talents, or tools?

_____
_____
_____

How could these approaches change the way your student's classmates receive and interact with them?

_____

_____

_____

Step 5. Won't... or Can't?

List the challenging attitude and behaviors of your tough nugget here:

_____

_____

_____

Now, read each challenging behavior you've listed and say, "It's not about me." This exercise is even more powerful if you sit with each one for a moment. Imagine the behavior. Visualize the situation and the emotions involved. Put yourself in that place and feel the pressure of the moment. Now that you are there, say aloud, "It's not about me."

How does it feel to know it's not about you? For many, it is relieving, freeing, and calming.

_____

_____

Does this practice support your self-regulation?

_____

_____

Are there times when it is easier not to take it personally? When would that be? Are there times when it is harder? What do those look like?

_____

_____

_____

What else can you do to remind yourself that the behavior in front of you is not about you?

_____

_____

_____

Go back to your list of challenging behaviors (p. 228) and consider the following questions.

Are any of your reactions to these behaviors about you? Are you being triggered because of your own history or insecurities?

_____

_____

_____

_____

You answered the following questions in Chapter 1. Hopefully that exercise helped you get a better understanding of yourself and your buttons. Now go through the activity again, specifically with your tough nugget in mind.

When was the last time I flipped my lid for reasons related to my tough nugget?
_____
_____
_____
_____

What behavior pushed my button?
_____
_____
_____
_____

What is the button? Why is that a button for me?
_____
_____
_____
_____

What can I do to make that button less sensitive?
_____
_____
_____
_____

List a few of your tough nugget's behaviors in the following table and consider what they might be communicating to you.

What Your Student's Behavior Might Be Communicating

Behavior	Possible Communication

What was completing the table on the previous page like for you?
_____
_____

Are you able to dig deep and put yourself in your tough nugget's shoes to see what might be behind the behavior?
_____
_____

How does this change how you view your student's behaviors?
_____
_____

Note: This takes practice. If you get stuck, you can consult with a friend or colleague who is especially good at staying calm and enjoying even the most challenging kids. Ask them, "How do you remain calm in the storm?" Record their responses and keep a running list of reframes that are most helpful for you here.

_____
_____
_____
_____
_____
_____
_____

Read through the list of skills in the following table and put a checkmark next to any that you believe your student is lagging in.

Checklist of Skills Students Need to Succeed

✓	Academic	✓	Social
	Reading		Empathy and compassion
	Processing speed (verbal or written)		Understanding other perspectives
	Math computation		Reading social cues
	Writing proficiency		Conflict resolution
✓	**Executive Functioning**		Self-advocacy/getting needs met
	Working memory		Negotiating needs
	Task initiation		Friendship/social skills
	Planning	✓	**Personal**
	Organization		Self-awareness
	Inhibitory/impulse control		Identifying emotions
	Flexibility		Regulation skills
	Study skills		Stop and think
	Time management		Linking actions to consequences
	Sustained attention		Delayed gratification and patience
	Transitioning activities or attention		Self-initiation skills

When your student fails to meet expectations, is it because they don't want to, or because they are not able to? Have you tried multiple motivational strategies without success? That is often the sign that your student *can't* meet the expectation for some reason, not that they *won't*. If you were to look at it through that lens, what undeveloped skill might be getting in the way of your student's success? Fill in the blank template that follows.

Your Student's Behaviors and Skills in Possible Need of Development

Behavior	Skill in Possible Need of Development

What do you notice/wonder?

_____
_____
_____
_____

How does this information give you a new view of your tough nugget's behaviors?

_____
_____
_____
_____

How does this information give you a new view of your tough nugget's needs?

_____
_____
_____
_____

How does this information give you a new view of your tough nugget's undeveloped skill(s)?

_____
_____
_____
_____

Step 6. Needsleuthing

Identify and record in the following table the behavior that you find most distressing, disruptive, and unhealthy in your tough nugget. Be clear about what the behavior is and how and when you observe it.

Peeling Back the Outer Leaves: Your Student's Behavior

Describe the behavior here. What is happening? Be specific.		
Frequency. How often does the behavior occur?	Intensity. How severe and/or disruptive is the behavior?	Duration. How long do the behavioral episodes last?

Analyze the "inner leaves" of your student in the following template. For the identified behavior, note what prompts the behavior (the antecedent) and the result of the behavior (the consequence).

Analyzing the Inner Leaves: Your Student

Behavior. What is the behavior observed?	
Antecedent. What precipitates the behavior?	Consequence. What happens after the behavior?

Look for patterns in the behavior. Recruit the support and input of fellow educators, counselors, prior teachers, administrators, parents, and guardians to capture a detailed picture of what's going on and why. The following questions may help:

Are there times when or places where the behavior occurs more frequently?

_____

_____

_____

Are there times when or places where the behavior never occurs?

_____

_____

_____

Does the behavior occur (or not occur) around certain people?

_____

_____

_____

(Considering escape/avoidance in particular) Does the behavior enable the student to postpone or avoid a demanding task or get out of an unwanted situation or interaction? To what extent do you observe this?

_____

_____

_____

(Considering attention seeking in particular) Does the behavior enable the student to gain peer or adult attention? To what extent do you observe this?

_____

_____

_____

(Considering tangible token in particular) Does the behavior enable the student to gain a preferred activity or item, such as a game or toy? To what extent do you observe this?

_____

_____

_____

(Considering sensory stimulation or avoidance in particular) Does the behavior provide positive stimulation or avoidance of unpleasant stimulation as an alternative to the student's lack of engagement in activities? To what extent do you observe this?

_____

_____

_____

Based on the totality of your observations, notes, interviews, and discussions, which of the four functions do you believe is propelling this particular behavior?

1. Escape/avoidance
2. Attention seeking
3. Tangible token
4. Sensory needs

Why do you think this is the primary function behind the behavior? What have you directly observed, what evidence have you collected, and what else makes you think this is the function driving the behavior?

_____

_____

_____

Physical Need

Your case: I believe this student's behavior is driven by an unmet physical need because…

_____

_____

Emotional Need

Your case: I believe this student's behavior is driven by an unmet emotional need because…

_____

_____

Relational Need

Your case: I believe this student's behavior is driven by an unmet relational need because…

_____

_____

Control Need

Your case: I believe this student's behavior is driven by an unmet control need because…

_____

_____

As you analyze the case you've made for each of the unmet needs, which argument do you find strongest? Which is most likely? Why do you think so?

_____

_____

_____

Which unmet need do you believe is most pressing? Which unmet need, when addressed immediately, might provide your student with the most powerful boost?

_____

_____

_____

Step 7. Trial and Error (and Trial and Success)

If your student's unmet need is physical, what regulation strategies might you add to the list on p. 161?

_____
_____
_____
_____

Consult with colleagues and consider other approaches. Why might they work?

_____
_____
_____
_____

If your student's unmet need is emotional, what regulation strategies might you add to the list on p. 162?

_____
_____
_____
_____

Consult with colleagues and consider other approaches. Why might they work?

_____

_____

_____

_____

If your student's unmet need is relational, what relationship strategies might you add to the list on pp. 163–164?

_____

_____

_____

_____

Consult with colleagues and consider other approaches. Why might they work?

_____

_____

_____

_____

If your student's unmet need is control, what responsibility strategies might you add to the list on pp. 164–165?

_____

_____

_____

_____

Consult with colleagues and consider other approaches. Why might they work?

_____

_____

_____

_____

In the "Intervention Plan for Your Student" form on the next page, plug in the strategy (or strategies) you're putting into place, including adequate detail to craft a concrete, deliberate plan to achieve success.

Intervention Plan for Your Student

Goal statement: What is the primary unmet need you're attempting to meet/address?

_____

Strategy What approach will you take?	**Metric** How will you determine whether the intervention is successful?	**Skills** What will you and/or the student need for this strategy to take hold?	**Motivation** How will you encourage the student to keep trying? How will you keep yourself motivated to stick with it?	**Resources** What support (e.g., people, materials, time, space) will you and your student need?	**Action Plan** What steps will you take to address the student's unmet need?
Strategy A:					
Strategy B:					

You can use the following form to collect data on your efforts and the student outcomes.

Data Collection Form

Student name: _____   Teacher name: _____

Date: _____

Likert scale: 1 = No success, 2 = Limited success,
3 = Mostly successful, 4 = Full success

Time	Context	Intervention attempted	Degree of success (Likert scale)	Anecdotal notes
			1 2 3 4	
			1 2 3 4	
			1 2 3 4	

Step 8. When Things Go Haywire: Response Strategies

Are you attuned to your tough nugget and able to see signs of struggle and escalation early?
_____
_____

What do you notice?
_____
_____

When do you see those signs?
_____
_____

How quickly do you take action?
_____
_____

What do you ignore?
_____
_____

What do you address?
_____
_____

Does the student respond differently depending on the timeliness of your intervention? If so, in what ways?

_____

_____

Do you find yourself making personality or character statements about your student (even in your own head)?

_____

_____

How do you (or can you) remind yourself to focus on the behavior, not the student?

_____

_____

_____

How calm are you when dealing with your tough nugget's behavior?

_____

_____

Can you see the need behind that behavior and maintain a high bar while also not getting your buttons pushed?

_____

_____

Do you offer choices and compromises so your student can have some power while you get your needs met too?

_____

_____

Some students need to be taught what a compromise is when they are calm. Does your student need to practice when both of you are calm?

_____

_____

How and when can you do this?

_____

_____

_____

At Level One, how does the student respond to playful engagement?

_____

_____

_____

Do you have a handful of phrases that might help you connect with your student?

_____

_____

_____

Would starting with lightness and a reminder of the expectation help your student feel less in trouble (and therefore less likely to be triggered)?

_____

_____

_____

At Level Two, how often do you give direction and correction from across the room?

_____

_____

Would it be helpful for your tough nugget if you moved closer and used a quieter, more private voice?

_____

_____

When you offer choices, how does your student respond?

_____

_____

Check your choices: Do you tend to offer two fair choices, or an ultimatum?
_____
_____

How is your student's response different depending on the nature of the choices?
_____
_____

When you include a time frame or walk away to give space, how does your student respond?
_____
_____

Is your student able to compromise? How does that play out?
_____
_____

How might you remind yourself to access these Level Two strategies on a regular basis?
_____
_____

At Level Three, how can you remind yourself to remain vigilant to signs of dysregulation (in your student and yourself)?
_____
_____

What are some words and phrases you could prepare in advance, should you need to pause the conversation and take a break?

_____

_____

What are some healthy, safe options for how and where your student can de-escalate and self-regulate? When can you practice this?

_____

_____

_____

Do you have a system for giving a time and place for a repair conversation?

_____

_____

Have you taught your students (and adult colleagues, too!) the tools for making an effective repair?

_____

_____

How often do you repair with your tough nugget?

_____

_____

Do you come back to your student, who may be mad at you for holding them accountable (or whom you have expressed frustration toward), and have a conversation and work on the repair with them?

_____

_____

Have you been too permissive with your tough nugget? Too regimented?

_____

_____

How are you balancing availability with accountability?

_____

_____

Jot down some ideas of what you can say when repairing with your tough nugget. What are some of the key messages you want to convey to your student when engaging in this essential step?

_____

_____

_____

_____

References

ABC News. (2017, February 1). Teacher has personalized handshakes with every one of his students. *ABC News*. https://abcnews.go.com/Lifestyle/teacher-personalized-handshakes-students/story?id=45190825

Blaustein, M., & Kinniburgh, K. (2010). *Treating traumatic stress in children and adolescents: How to foster resilience through attachment, self-regulation, and competency*. Guilford.

Blaustein, M. E., & Kinniburgh, K. M. (2017). Attachment, self-regulation, and competency (ARC). In M. A. Landolt, M. Cloitre, & U. Schnyder (Eds.), *Evidence-based treatments for trauma related disorders in children and adolescents* (pp. 299–319). Springer International Publishing/Springer Nature.

Cohen, G. (2022). *Belonging: The science of creating connection and bridging divides*. W. W. Norton.

Duhigg, C. (2014). *The power of habit: Why we do what we do in life and business*. Random House.

Erickson, K. I., Leckie, R. L., & Weinstein, A. M. (2014, May 14). Physical activity, fitness, and gray matter volume. *Neurobiology of Aging*, S20–S28.

Felitti, V. J., Anda, R. F., Nordenberg, D., Williamson, D. F., Spitz, A. M., Edwards, V., Koss, M. P., & Marks, J. S. (1998). Relationship of childhood abuse and household dysfunction to many of the leading causes of death in adults: The Adverse Childhood Experiences (ACE) Study. *American Journal of Preventive Medicine, 14*(4), 245–258.

Gopalan, M., & Brady, S. T. (2020). College students' sense of belonging: A national perspective. *Educational Researcher, 49*(2), 134–137.

Gray, C. A., & Garand, J. D. (1993, April). Social stories: Improving responses of students with autism with accurate social information. *Focus on Autistic Behavior, 8*(1), 1–10.

Greene, R. (2009). *Lost at school: Why our kids with behavioral challenges are falling through the cracks at school and how we can help them.* Scribner.

Griffin, Z. A. M., Boulton, K. A., Thapa, R., DeMayo, M. M., Ambarchi, Z., Thomas, E., Pokorski, I., Hickie, I. E., & Guastella, A. J. (2022, March 17). Atypical sensory processing features in children with autism, and their relationships with maladaptive behaviors and caregiver strain. *Autism Research, 15*(6), 1120–1129.

Hall, P. (2019, March 4). Healthy brains? It's up to you! [Blog post]. *Fostering Resilient Learners.* www.fosteringresilientlearners.org/blog/2019/4/8/healthy

Harvard Health Publishing. (2021, August 14). Giving thanks can make you happier. *Harvard Health Publishing.* www.health.harvard.edu/healthbeat/giving-thanks-can-make-you-happier

Harvard Health Publishing. (2024, April 3). Foods linked to better brainpower. *Harvard Health Publishing.* http://health.harvard.edu/healthbeat/foods-linked-to-better-brainpower

Hattie, J. (2023). *Visible learning: The sequel: A synthesis of over 2,100 meta-analyses relating to achievement.* Routledge.

Inman, C. S., Hollearn, M. K., Augustin, L., Campbell, J. M., Olson, K. L., & Wahlstrom, K. L. (2023, November 7). Discovering how the amygdala shapes human behavior: From lesion studies to neuromodulation. *Neuron, 111*(24), 3906–3910.

Jerath, R., Edry, J. W., Barnes, V. A., & Jerath, V. (2006, April 18). Physiology of long pranayamic breathing: Neural respiratory elements may provide a mechanism that explains how slow deep breathing shifts the autonomic nervous system. *Medical Hypotheses, 67*(3), 566–571.

Jha, A., Diehl, B., Strange, B., Miserocchi, A., Chowdhury, F., McEvoy, A. W., & Nachev, P. (2023, January). Orienting to fear under transient focal disruption of the human amygdala. *Brain, 146*(1), 135–148.

Knoster, T. (1991). *Factors in managing complex change.* Presentation at TASH Conference, Washington, DC.

Lally, P., van Jaarsveld, C. H. M., Potts, H. W. W., & Wardle, J. (2010). How are habits formed: Modelling habit formation in the real world. *European Journal of Social Psychology, 40*(6), 998–1009.

LeDoux, J. E. (1996). *The emotional brain: The mysterious underpinnings of emotional life*. Simon & Schuster.

Madden G. (Ed.). (2013). *APA handbook of behavior analysis*. American Psychological Association.

Mayo Clinic Staff. (2023, September 22). Stress relief from laughter? It's no joke [Blog post]. *Mayo Clinic Healthy Lifestyle*. www.mayoclinic.org/healthy-lifestyle/stress-management/in-depth/stress-relief/art-20044456

Moore, S. (2019). What is neuronal plasticity and why is it important? *News-Medical.Net*. https://www.news-medical.net/life-sciences/What-is-Neuronal-Plasticity-and-Why-Is-It-Important.aspx

Muppalla, S. K., Vuppalapati, S., Reddy Pulliahgaru, A., & Sreenivasulu, H. (2023, June 18). Effects of excessive screen time on child development: An updated review and strategies for management. *Cureus, 15*(6), e40608.

Orchard, K., & Souers, K. (2020, February 17). Culture of safety element 2 of 3: Predictability [Blog post]. *Fostering Resilient Learners*. www.fosteringresilientlearners.org/blog/2020/2/17/culture-of-safety-element-2-of-3-predictable

Osika, A., MacMahon, S., Lodge, J. M., & Carroll, A. (2022, March 18). Emotions and learning: What role do emotions play in how and why students learn? *Times Higher Education*. www.timeshighereducation.com/campus/emotions-and-learning-what-role-do-emotions-play-how-and-why-students-learn

Phelps, E. A., & LeDoux, J. E. (2005). Contributions of the amygdala to emotion processing: From animal models to human behavior. *Neuron, 48*(2), 175–187.

Pierson, R. F. (2013, May). *Every kid needs a champion* [Video]. TED Talks Education. https://www.ted.com/talks/rita_pierson_every_kid_needs_a_champion

Psychology Today staff. (n.d.). Empathy. *Psychology Today*. https://www.psychologytoday.com/gb/basics/empathy

Purvis, K. B., Cross, D. R., Dansereau, D. F., & Parris, S. R. (2013, December 17). Trust-Based Relational Intervention (TBRI): A systemic approach to complex developmental trauma. *Child and Youth Services, 34*(4), 360–386.

Purvis, K. B., Cross, D. R., & Sunshine, W. L. (2007). *The connected child: Bring hope and healing to your adoptive family*. McGraw-Hill Professional.

Rowe, A., & Souers, K. (2020, February 17). Culture of safety element 1 of 3: Safety [Blog post]. *Fostering Resilient Learners*. www.fosteringresilientlearners.org/blog/2020/2/17/culture-of-safety-element-1-of-3-safe

Savage, B. M., Lujan, H. L., Thipparthi, R. R., & DiCarlo, S. E. (2017, July 5). Humor, laughter, learning, and health! A brief review. *Advances in Physiology Education*. https://journals.physiology.org/doi/full/10.1152/advan.00030.2017

Shabir, O. (2020, September 16). Levels of hydration and cognitive function. *News-Medical.Net*. https://www.news-medical.net/health/Levels-of-Hydration-and-Cognitive-Function.aspx

Shehata, M., Cheng, M., Leung, A., Tsuchiya, N., Wu, D-A., Tseng, C-h., Nakauchi, S., & Shimojo, S. (2021, October 4). Team flow is a unique brain state associated with enhanced information integration and interbrain synchrony. *eNeuro, 8*(5).

Siegel, D. (2017). *Dr. Dan Siegel's hand model of the brain* [Video]. YouTube. https://www.youtube.com/watch?v=f-m2YcdMdFw

Siegel, D. J., & Bryson, T. P. (2011). *The whole-brain child: 12 revolutionary strategies to nurture your child's developing mind*. Delacorte.

Singh, B., Murphy, A., Maher, C., & Smith, A. E. (2024, December 9). Time to form a habit: A systematic review and meta-analysis of health behaviour habit formation and its determinants. *Healthcare (Basel), 12*(23), 2488.

Souers, K. (2024). *10 things our brains need* (B. Cook, Illus.). Fostering Resilient Learners.

Souers, K. (with Hall, P.). (2016). *Fostering resilient learners: Strategies for creating a trauma-sensitive classroom*. ASCD.

Turner, W. (2019, April 8). Rubber bracelets to support emotional regulation? Absolutely! [Blog post]. *Fostering Resilient Learners*. www.fosteringresilientlearners.org/blog/2019/4/8/rubber-bracelets-to-support-emotional-regulation-absolutely

Turner, W. (2023). *Embracing adult SEL: An educator's guide to personal social emotional learning success*. Routledge.

Turner, W., & Souers, K. (2020, February 17). Culture of safety element 3 of 3: Consistency [Blog post]. *Fostering Resilient Learners*. www.fosteringresilientlearners.org/blog/2020/2/17/culture-of-safety-element-3-of-3-consistency

van der Kolk, B. (2015). *The body keeps the score: Brain, body, and mind in the healing of trauma*. Penguin.

Van Marter Souers, K. (with Hall, P.). (2019). *Relationship, responsibility, and regulation: Trauma-invested practices for fostering resilient learners*. ASCD.

Van Marter Souers, K., & Hall, P. (2018). *Creating a trauma-sensitive classroom* (Quick reference guide). ASCD.

Van Marter Souers, K., & Hall, P. (2019). *Trauma-invested practices to meet students' needs* (Quick reference guide). ASCD.

Wexler, D. B. (2020). *The stop program: Handouts and homework*. W. W. Norton.

Whalen, P. J., Rauch, S. L., Etcoff, N. L., McInerney, S. C., Lee, M. B., & Jenike, M. A. (2001). Masked presentations of emotional facial expressions modulate amygdala activity without explicit knowledge. *The Journal of Neuroscience, 18*(1), 411–418.

Xie, L., Kang, H., Xu, Q., Chen, M. J., Liao, C., Thiyagarajan, M., O'Donnell, J., Christensen, D. J., Nicholson, C., Iliff, J. J., Takano, T., Deane, R., & Nedergaard, M. (2013, October 18). Sleep drives metabolite clearance from the adult brain. *Science, 342*(6156), 373–377.

Zemeckis, R. (Director). (1994). *Forrest Gump* [Film]. Paramount Pictures.

Index

Note: Page references followed by an italicized *f* indicate information contained in figures.

academic skills for success, 141*f*
accountability, 28, 166
accountability strategies, 81–82
activity tracker, weeklong, 69*f*–70*f*
adult culture of safety, 71–74
adult leadership for proactive relationships, 40–41
affirmations, positive, 163
anger, 137
antecedent analysis, 148–151
    behavior functions, 147–148
apologizing, 52, 192
applied behavior analysis
attention-seeking behaviors, 148
auditing your nest, 36–38, 37*f*–38*f*
availability strategies, 83–84, 166
avoidance behaviors, 148

behavior, student
    about, 75–76
    accountability strategies, 81–82

behavior, student—(*continued*)
    antecedent analysis, 148–151
    availability strategies, 83–84
    balanced approach to, 75, 78–81, 78*f*, 84–85
    catch behavior early, 176–178
    as communication, 59–60, 136–140
    discipline, 87–88
    focus on behavior, not person, 178–180
    functions of, 147–148
    helpful-healthy-safe triad, 76–77, 76*f*, 78*f*
    Jot Your Thoughts, 80
    Pause and Reflect, 81, 82, 86
    permissiveness, 79, 81
    Pete's experience, 86
    regimentation and rule adherence, 79, 82
    summary questions, 89
body/mind control, 61–62
boundaries, setting intentional, 20, 72

brain breaks, 32
brain health, 65–68, 145
brain language, 162
brain nutrition, 66, 69f
breathing, 162
breathing, mindful, 20
breathing exercises, 32, 66, 69f
buttons, knowing your, 17, 19–20

Caleb (case study student)
    avoid power struggles, 182–183
    background and historical research and fieldwork, 102–103
    behavior observation, 146
    catch behavior early, 177
    check in with Ms. Coombs, 109
    connection strategy implementation, 125
    culture of safety audit, 111, 114–116
    focus on behavior, not person, 179, 180f
    fostering connections, 118–120, 125
    intervention data collection, 171f–173f
    intervention plan, 167f–168f
    levels of response, 183–191
    listing strengths and positive attributes, 98–100
    needs determination analysis, 153–154, 156–158
    peer relationships, 127–128
    reframing behaviors, 131–132, 135–136, 138, 142
    repair and restore relationship, 192–195

Caleb (case study student)—(*continued*)
    skill development, 142
    specific behaviors and issues to address, 105–106
    team approach, 201–203
calming corners, 32
calming engagement, 190–192
case study student. *See* Caleb (case study student)
cement shoes, 13–14, 32–33
challenge, 66–67, 69f
championing every student, 50–51
check-ins, 46, 68, 122
choice, student, 31, 164, 187
clarity of purpose, 35
classroom management model. *See also* discipline; intervention plans
    about, 75–76
    accountability strategies, 81–82
    availability strategies, 83–84
    balanced approach to, 75, 78–81, 78f, 84–85
    discipline, 87–88
    helpful-healthy-safe triad, 76–77, 76f, 78f
    Jot Your Thoughts, 80
    menu of strategies, 161–165
    Pause and Reflect, 81, 82, 86
    permissiveness, 79, 81
    Pete's experience, 86
    regimentation and rule adherence, 79, 82
    summary questions, 89
classroom setup, 30–31

common language use, 35
communication
    behavior as, 59–60, 136–140
    and predictability, 30
    signals and visuals to support students', 32
    six steps for effective, 192
community agreements, 30
community-building activities audit, 44f–45f
compliments, 163
compromise, 188
confidence, 82
conflict, facing head-on, 82
connections, fostering, 40
    adult leadership for proactive relationships, 40–41
    championing every student, 50–51
    empathy, 48–49, 122
    Jot Your Thoughts, 47, 53
    Keith's experience, 43
    Kristin's experience, 47–48
    liked vs. respected, 41–43
    peer relationships, 127–129
    positive behavior reinforcement, 122–123
    positivity-to-negativity ratio, 123
    proactive relationships strategies audit, 44f–45f
    relationship-building strategies, 45–47
    repair, 51–53, 123
    social stories, 49
    strategies for tough nuggets, 122–123

connections, fostering—(*continued*)
    student-teacher proactive relationships, 43–44
    summary questions, 89
consent across the board, 35
consistency, 34–35
    clarity of purpose, 35
    common language use, 35
    consent across the board, 35
    expectations, 35–36
    follow-through, 36
    in intervention plan, 175
control
    boundary setting, 20
    classroom setup and student choice, 31
    is a myth, 83
    locus of control exercise, 21–22, 21f
control need, 60, 61f, 154, 164–165
core-building exercises, 32
criticism, sensitivity to, 18
culture of safety, 11, 27, 36
    auditing your nest, 36–38, 37f–38f
    consistency in environment, 34–36
    dysregulated students, 32–33
    emotional safety, 28
    Jot Your Thoughts, 29, 34
    Pete's experience, 32–33
    physical safety, 28
    plans and expectations to reestablish, 28–29
    predictability, 29–34
    strengthening adult, 71–74
    summary questions, 89

data collection, intervention, 169–173, 170*f*
deep-breathing exercises, 32, 162
defiance, 137
discipline. *See also* classroom management model; intervention plans
    avoid power struggles, 180–183
    catch behavior early, 176–178
    five keys to, 81, 176*f*
    focus on behavior, not person, 178–180
    implementing, 86–87
    levels of response, 183–192
    reflecting on your style of, 87–88
    repair and restore relationships, 192–195
distractors, 161
downstairs brain/upstairs brain, 32–33, 35
dysregulation, 23, 32–33, 61–63, 190

elementary safety survey, 37*f*–38*f*
emotional need, 59, 61*f*, 154, 162–163
emotional support, 40–41. *See also* connections, fostering
emotions, identifying, 83–84, 162
empathy, 25, 48–49, 122
environment design, 30–31, 161, 165
escalating, 162
escape/avoidance behaviors, 148
event attendance, 46
executive functioning skills for success, 141*f*
exercise, 66, 69*f*
expectations, consistent, 35–36, 72, 165

eye contact, 47, 163

family communication, 46, 68
focus, 21
follow-through, 36, 200–201
forecast changes, 30
Functional Family Therapy, 43

game playing, 46
gratitude, 67, 70*f*
greeting students, 122
groundedness, 13–14

habits, brain health, 68
hand model of the brain, 17
handshakes, 46–47
helpful-healthy-safe triad of behavior, 76–77, 76*f*, 78*f*
high fives, 46–47
hugs, 46–47
hydration, 66, 69*f*, 161

immune system, 67
insecurity, 18
intentional wording, 47
intervention plans. *See also* classroom management model; discipline; Your Turn (tough nugget plan development)
    about, 160
    avoid power struggles, 180–183
    catch behavior early, 176–178
    data collection, 169–173, 170*f*
    focus on behavior, not person, 178–180

intervention plans—(*continued*)
    implementation, 166–168, 166*f*
    levels of response, 183–192
    menu of strategies, 161–165
    repair and restore relationships, 192–195
    responding to setbacks or ineffectiveness, 175–176

laughter, 67, 70*f*
lid flips, 17
liked *vs.* respected, 41–43
locus of control exercise, 21–22, 21*f*

meetings, problem-solving, 198–200
mind/body control, 61–62
mindful breathing, 20
mindfulness meditation, 32, 161
mindset, reframing, 22–25, 23*f*, 83
mission statement, personal, 16
modeling self-regulation, 17
morning meetings, 46
movement, 161

names, student, 45
needs, basic. *See also* wellness
    and behavior, 59–60, 153–159
    intervention based on unmet, 161–165
    universal strategies to meet students', 60, 61*f*
needsleuthing
    about, 145–146
    applied behavior analysis, 147–153
    observation and note-taking, 146–147

needsleuthing—(*continued*)
    pinpointing ultimate driver of behavior, 153–159
negative mindsets, 40–41
negative thought reframing, 23*f*
nests, safe and trauma-invested
    auditing your nest, 36–38, 37*f*–38*f*
    overview, 11–12
neuronal plasticity, 66–67
nicknames, 45–46
norms and expectations, 30
noticing individual student changes, 46
nutrition, 66, 69*f*, 161

observation and attunement, 46, 190
"our" mentality *vs.* "my" mentality, 72

peer relationships, 127–129, 137
perfectionism, 18
permission to ask questions, 72
permissiveness, 79, 81
personal mission, 16
personal skills for success, 141*f*
physical need, 59, 61*f*, 153, 161–162
physical proximity, 186
physical touch, 46–47, 163
planning and practicing, 30
playful engagement, 184–186
positive affirmations, 163
positive behavior reinforcement, 122–123
positive reframes, 23*f*
positive shout-outs, 72

positivity-to-negativity ratio, 123
power struggles, avoid, 180–183
praise, 163
pranayama breathing, 66
predictability, 29
    communication, 30
    community agreements, 30
    forecast changes, 30
    healthy rituals, 31
    planning and practicing, 30
    self-regulation, 31–32
    space design, 30–31
primary safety survey, 37*f*
proactive relationships. *See* connections, fostering
proactive relationships strategies audit, 44*f*–45*f*
professional development, 81
proximity, 186

questioning, permission for, 72

reframing, 22–25, 23*f*
    behavior as communication, 59–60, 136–140
    mind/body control, 61–62, 140–143, 141*f*
    not about you, 58–59, 131–136
refusing to work, 137
regimentation and rule adherence, 79, 82
regulation, 23
regulation reset options, 32
reinforcing positive behaviors, 122–123
relational need, 59–60, 61*f*, 154, 163–164

Relationship, Responsibility, and Regulation (Van Marter Souers with Hall), 23, 161
relationship-building strategies, 45–47
repairing relationships, 51–53, 68, 123, 164, 192–195
reset spaces, 162, 163, 164
respect *vs.* liking, 41–43
response levels, discipline
    about, 183–184
    calming engagement, 190–192
    playful engagement, 184–186
    structured engagement, 186–190
responsibility, modeling, 52, 192
rituals, healthy, 31
routines, healthy, 31

safety, culture of. *See* culture of safety
saying "no," 20
saying students' names, 45
screen time, 67, 69*f*
seating options, 161, 165
self. *See* You
self-care challenge, 69*f*–70*f*
self-regulation, student. *See also* behavior, student
    behavior issues and, 131, 162
    dysregulation, 23, 32–33, 61–63, 190
self-regulation, teacher, 16–17
    Keith's experience, 17–18
    knowing your buttons, 19–20
    and predictability, 31–32
    promoting and teaching, 32
sensory needs behaviors, 148

shout-outs, 72
shutting down, 137
skills needed for success, 141*f*
sleep, 65, 69*f*, 161
social connectedness among staff, 71
social skills for success, 141*f*
social stories, 49
soft voice, 187
space design, 30–31
staff celebrations, 71
staff social connectedness, 71
stimulation behaviors, 148
stress. *See* trauma and stress
stressors, self-regulation and, 16–20
    focus, 21
    mindful, deep breathing, 20
    setting intentional boundaries, 20
structured engagement, 186–190
student behavior. *See* behavior, student; Your Turn (tough nugget plan development)
student case study. *See* Caleb (case study student)
student choice, 31, 164, 187
student involvement in behavioral intervention plans, 151–152
student names, 45
student needs. *See* needs, basic; need-sleuthing; wellness
student self-regulation. *See also* behavior, student
    behavior issues and, 131, 162
    dysregulation, 23, 32–33, 61–63, 190
students, greeting, 122
students, welcoming, 31
success, mental vision of, 165
succinctness, 190–191
systems of meaning, reframing, 22–25, 23*f*

tangible token behaviors, 148
"tap-in, tap-out" protocols, 72, 73–74
teacher self-regulation, 16–17
    Keith's experience, 17–18
    knowing your buttons, 19–20
    and predictability, 31–32
    promoting and teaching, 32
teacher-student proactive relationships, 43–44
teachers. *See* You
team approach
    about, 197
    case study, 201–203
    follow through, 200–201
    intentional meetings, 198–200
    membership, 198
    plan creation, 200
teamwork, 66, 69*f*, 72
threat, 185
time frames for response, 188
tool belt, 81
tough nugget plan development. *See* Your Turn (tough nugget plan development)
transitions, 162
trauma and stress
    behavior is communication, 59–60, 136–140
    body/mind control, 61–62, 140–143

trauma and stress—(*continued*)
    effects on brain, 55–58
    Jot Your Thoughts, 62–63
    Pete's experience, 57–58
    reactions to, 58–59, 131–136
    summary questions, 89
    universal strategies to meet students' needs, 60, 61*f*
    won't *vs.* can't, 61
trust, rebuilding, 28
Trust-Based Relational Intervention, 81, 184
2x10 strategy, 46, 122

vulnerability, 28

water, 66, 69*f*, 161
weeklong activity tracker, 69*f*–70*f*
welcoming students, 31
wellness
    factors for a strong brain, 65–68
    Jot Your Thoughts, 70–71, 73
    Kristin's experience, 73–74
    self-care challenge, 69*f*–70*f*
    strengthening adult culture of safety, 71–74
    summary questions, 89

yoga, 32
You
    enhancing self-regulation skills, 20–22
    Jot Your Thoughts, 14–15, 24–25
    Keith's experience, 17–18

You—(*continued*)
    knowing your buttons, 17, 19–20
    Kristin's experience, 25
    locus of control exercise, 21–22, 21*f*
    overview, 13
    Pause and Reflect, 22
    personal mission, 16
    reframing, 22–25, 23*f*, 131–132
    self-knowledge, 13–15
    self-regulation, 16–20
    summary questions, 89
"You're Awesome" bag, 47–48
Your Turn (tough nugget plan development)
    avoid power struggles, 180–181
    background and historical research and fieldwork, 103–104
    behavior functional analysis, 152–153
    behavior observation, 147
    catch behavior early, 177–178
    check in with yourself, 107–108, 110
    connection strategy implementation, 123–124, 126
    culture of safety audit, 111–113, 116
    focus on behavior, not person, 178–179
    fostering connections, 120–121, 122–123
    implementation data collection, 169, 170*f*
    intervention plan implementation, 166*f*
    intervention strategy menu, 161–165
    levels of response, 183–192

Your Turn (tough nugget plan development)—(*continued*)
    listing strengths and positive attributes, 100–102
    needs determination analysis, 153–155, 158–159
    peer relationships, 128–129
    reframing behaviors, 131, 132–135, 139–140, 142–143
    repair and restore relationship, 192–195
    skill development, 143
    specific behaviors and issues to address, 106

About the Authors

Kristin Van Marter Souers is a licensed mental-health clinician and has more than 30 years of experience teaching, coaching, training, and consulting in a multitude of settings. She is the lead author (with Pete Hall) of two revolutionary, best-selling books on childhood trauma and stress: *Fostering Resilient Learners: Strategies for Creating a Trauma-Sensitive Classroom* and *Relationship, Responsibility, and Regulation: Trauma-Invested Practices for Fostering Resilient Learners*. She is also the author of the first in a series of children's books to come: *10 Things Our Brains Need*. Her next book (title and release date to be determined) delves even further into this work.

Keith Orchard is an experienced social worker and the current mental health facilitator in the Coeur d'Alene School District in Idaho. He brings his background as a Peace Corps volunteer, educator, youth ranch coordinator, family counselor on a Marine Corps base, and sports coach to this project. Keith has worked alongside Kristin and Pete in providing professional development and coaching support to educators since 2018. This workbook is the culmination of many discussions among the three authors in connection with the work they do to address the needs of students who struggle.

Pete Hall is an award-winning school principal and author or coauthor of 12 books, including *Fostering Resilient Learners* and *Relationship, Responsibility, and Regulation* with Kristin Van Marter Souers and his recent social psychology life guide, *Always Strive to Be a Better You: How Ordinary People Can Live Extraordinary Lives*. He has worked in education for 30 years and provided professional development support to educators across the globe.

Related ASCD Resources

At the time of publication, the following resources were available (ASCD stock numbers appear in parentheses).

Creating a Trauma-Sensitive Classroom (Quick Reference Guide) by Kristin Van Marter Souers and Pete Hall (#QRG118054)

Every Connection Matters: How to Build, Maintain, and Restore Relationships Inside the Classroom and Out by Michael Creekmore and Nita Creekmore (#123010)

Fostering Resilient Learners: Strategies for Creating a Trauma-Sensitive Classroom by Kristin Van Marter Souers with Pete Hall (#116014)

Meet Their Needs, and They'll Succeed: Transforming Students' Lives Through Positive Relationships by Salome Thomas-El (#121003)

Powerful Student Care: Honoring Each Learner as Distinctive and Irreplaceable by Grant Chandler and Kathleen M. Budge (#123009)

Relationship, Responsibility, and Regulation: Trauma-Invested Practices for Fostering Resilient Learners by Kristin Van Marter Souers with Pete Hall (#119027)

Teaching with Empathy: How to Transform Your Practice by Understanding Your Learners by Lisa Westman (#121027)

Trauma-Informed Teaching and IEPs: Strategies for Building Student Resilience by Melissa Sadin (#122026)

Trauma-Invested Practices to Meet Students' Needs (Quick Reference Guide) by Kristin Van Marter Souers and Pete Hall (#QRG119077)

Trauma-Responsive Educational Practices: Helping Students Cope and Learn by Micere Keels (#122015)

Trauma-Sensitive School Leadership: Building a Learning Environment to Support Healing and Success by Bill Ziegler, Dave Ramage, Andrea Parson, and Justin Foster (#122013)

For up-to-date information about ASCD resources, go to **www.ascd.org**. You can search the complete archives of *Educational Leadership* at **www.ascd.org/el**. To contact us, send an email to member@ascd.org or call 1-800-933-2723 or 703-578-9600.

DON'T MISS A SINGLE ISSUE OF THIS AWARD-WINNING MAGAZINE.

iste+ascd
educational leadership

If you belong to a Professional Learning Community, you may be looking for a way to get your fellow educators' minds around a complex topic. Why not delve into a relevant theme issue of *Educational Leadership*, the journal written by educators for educators?

Subscribe now and browse or purchase back issues of our flagship publication at **www.ascd.org/el**. Discounts on bulk purchases are available.

iste+ascd

Arlington, VA USA
1-800-933-2723

www.ascd.org
www.iste.org

www.ingramcontent.com/pod-product-compliance
Lightning Source LLC
Chambersburg PA
CBHW060537010526
44119CB00052B/745